STILL
THE RIVERS
FLOWED

MARK HURST

INTRODUCTION

I have no idea why I started writing poetry. Junior year in High School we studied poetry including the greats, Robert Frost, Carl Sandberg, Dylan Thomas, and Paul Simon.

Mrs. Wray taught us that poetry is poetry even in modern folk songs, rock and roll, or "written on the subway walls and tenement halls, and written in the sounds of silence." She made us memorize and recite poetry. We tried, with little success, to understand Haiku. She required us to write a poem. That was the last time I gave it a try.

Fifty years later I tried again. It was just as bad.

Some of the ideas, some of the rhymes in this collection came to me, a brick out of the sky. Others I had to go looking for. Writing is my creative outlet and poetry is my muse, Calliope, whispering in my ear. She is probably disgusted with the confused rants, the tangled logic, the unsophisticated pentameter.

Whatever.

MARK

ABOUT THE AUTHOR

This is the guy who, at age six had to be pulled out of the deep end of a swimming pool three times before the life guard tossed him over the fence into the kiddie pool.

This is the guy who famously said he'd never own a cell phone.

This is the guy who thought it would be a good idea to buy a diesel engine car in the middle of the oil wars of the 80's but realized too late that the only diesel powered cars at the time were Oldsmobiles, the ad agency for which famously tried to convince us, "this is not your father's Oldsmobile." It was.

This is the guy who decided to leave city life and buy a bunch of land and become a gentleman farmer. He has yet to eat a ripe tomato, donating virtually all the produce to the local deer population.

This is the guy who thought he might like to try writing a little poetry to make him sound cool, hip, wise.

Good luck

MH

1
NO EXCUSES

I sat and told my story to my best friend,
Who patiently listened all the way to the bitter end.
And when I asked for her best advice
She said, "You may want to think about it twice."
You'll never make it in this world so just pretend.

There is, there was, an innocence of youth,
But it vanished without explanation or excuse.
"Innocence," my friend cried aloud,
"Some things are simply not allowed,
Especially if they take you further from the truth."

There was the phony personality I purloined,
Snappy repartee, quotable phrases cleverly coined.
There was a painful voice in a fragile, ancient book,
A constant reminder of all the abuse I took,
And the off-key, hallelujah chorus I joined.

My friend urged, "When you've found love's lost abode,
Marked the trails you blazed, the footpaths you strode,
When you've seen the final curve, the last horizon,
Hear distant rhythms of unrecognized bygones
Remember the strong ones on whose shoulders you rode.

My deep convictions, naively resolute,
Left me, twisted, tangled, intellectually destitute.
My friend advised, "Lie down in a shallow grave,
Silently cover up the mess you made,
Enjoy the darkness, blind, and mute."

With her tendency to heartlessly upbraid,
She drew from me all the unforced errors I made.
As we talked, she took a caustic jab
At the heartfelt conversations I thought we'd had,
Her winning hand, in the end, badly overplayed.

With timely deployment of her biting wit,
Flawed logic, a twisting posit,
"Take your time," she wisely advised,
"There's nothing left for you to hide,"
Now I'm desperate to make some sense of it.

I urged, "Be honest," but still she spoke in code.
"Help me find the strength to lift my heavy load,"
I begged as she closed the book.
The thunder clapped, the mountains shook,
And still the rivers flowed.

2

PLEIN AIRE

The oils flow effortlessly,
At dawn,
With its fleeting, orange spectrum,
 Morning darkness reluctantly moves along.
With an imperceptible push, Bristle on canvas,
A quiet shush,
A subtle scrape,
The reverent whisper of my brush.
Morning and its morning colors
Greet me, welcome me,
And I envy Its casual crawl,
A lazy roll, no hurry,
No deadline, no pressure, no rush.

The colors blend and mix,
Raw sienna, burnt umber, cobalt blue,
And glisten in this amber glow,
Awakened in the early, lonely hours
To reveal their secret, undiscovered hues,
From colors I'd never seen before,
Only thought I knew.
Here in this meadow, en plein-air,
With ample time to think,

Little time to spare.

Now, the balky brush decides

Its own vision, its own strokes,

And doesn't much care

What I see,

What I think I see,

What I want to see,

Hope I see.

The brush will not move,

Will not give way,

Will not cooperate

Or see things the way

My eye would choose,

Or the way nature would approve.

The colors are all wrong

,The strokes are not mine,

They belong to someone else,

Some other unseen artist, insistent, strong,

Who controls the shadows, the light,

And gives no instructions,

Offers no excuse

Nor kind rebuke,

But holds its place

Even as my feeble efforts

See the colors turn a muddy gray

And wish they could erase,

Start again, wash away.

Now comes the heat.

Comes the rain,

Comes a summer torrent,

Comes the disappointment.

O my dismay

The final work will be delayed,

The en plein aire magic I was hoping to find

Would have to wait

For a second chance, another day.

And there would be more days,

More weeks, more months, more eons,

Vanished in the haze. A million ticks of the clock,

Ten thousand brush strokes Ten thousand again,

And yet again,

The brush will not let me wander,

Mother nature won't let me find her.

No place to stop

No place to begin, or end,

Or start over.

So, my strokes become violent,

Unforgiving, harsh,

Part of the painful past,

A cruel reminder.

My brush now a rapier--

Parry, thrust, lunge--

A knife, a sword, a machete

And all the colors,

The reds, the yellows, and greens

Are resolute, firm, unwavering

And will not let me paint the scene
Until I stop seeing pieces,
And learn to see the whole.
Until my tears splash the palette,
Until I find its soul.

Thirty years have passed,
The city, the concrete,
The brick, and the glass,
And the chaos, and the noise,
And the madness of the city--
Bedlam amassed--
Have left me fragile, broken, confined,
And the information age,
With its dreamy, googley eyes,
Has finally crashed.
I won't get back the years I lost,
They're gone, And I am gone,
Unable to calculate the burden or the cost.
Unwilling to quantify the sweat, the toil
Knowing there is still a place--
I hope there is still a place--
The scene I long ago failed to capture,
Pray it is unchanged, unspoiled.
Let me take up, once again
Stiffened brushes,
Wobbly tripod legs,
Aging oils.

As I unpack my tools,

My anger, and my regrets,
From my well-worn, leather valise,
The air is clean, my thoughts are clear,
I am unshackled,
Unburdened, released.
There is harmony in the air,
All the static has ceased,
The trees reach out to touch me,
The river waves, a silent hush,
And I have found solitude,
A certain and unfamiliar peace.
And now I know
That you expose light by creating shadow,
Painting, not just what you see,
Not simply what you want,
But what you know,
What you feel.
I stand in this sanctuary
And, as the dawn hours beckon,
I pause in the morning light
And kneel.
And weep.
And now the oils,
Once again, begin to flow.
I have given up the fight.
As the mountain air cools me,
Lifts me, carries me away
From my burdens on the ground below.

My senses all take flight,
The effortless movement
Of a passion I once knew,
Awash in thin-air mountain light,
Once again begins to show.
I have found comfort here,
At last, an inner calm
And the painting that eluded me,
(Passion I thought dead in me.)
The unfinished painting that denuded me,
Would not let me forget,
Would not cease.
In the quiet of the morning
I can feel the rhythm of redemption,
The symphony of the weary,
And in my calloused hand
My brush is a conductor's baton
That moves to a faint, rhythmic beat,
Then stroke by stroke,
By painful Parkinsonian stroke,
And to my eternal relief,
The feeble effort, somehow grew
Into a plein-air masterpiece.

"Immature poets imitate; mature poets steal."

T.S. ELLIOT

3
FINAL EPITAPH

You were a budding dancer when we met
Though I never saw you on the stage,
Or took the time to see you turn a single pirouette,
Just another detail lost from the scrap-book page.
Add it to the growing list, one more thing to regret.

We convinced ourselves, in time, that nothing is built to last,
And buckled highways left us mostly lost,
A heartbreak for these children of the working class.
Our minds were clear and our spirits washed,
Now there's not a single relic of our painful past.

Our radical wants, our restless ways,
Yielded to all things simple and mundane.
The sunsets we watched, the way we were taught to pray,
Wondering if we would stay exactly the same,
Or become cowards and run away.

I left no parting note, there was no tearful goodbye,
Afraid of being cornered, caged, and caught,
With courage in very short supply.
I'm still listening for your best parting shot
As twilight hours now quickly pass me by.

These were the years of uncertainty,
And our longings had to be pushed aside.
Before we could comprehend love's volatility
I walked away with a surfeit of pride
And a glaring inanition of humility.

It may have been number twenty-five—
Though that may be, in the end, a feeble excuse—
Trying to stay relevant, desperate to stay alive
But ended up frighteningly obtuse,
Spiritually drained, emotionally deprived.

There was a spark, a flame, a blaze that burned me,
Wildlife came running from the uncontrolled fire,
In a moment where bravery eluded me
I became an apologist, far worse a liar.
Courage never looked good on me.

I'm not sure it was passion I lacked,
Just an ugly disregard, most days, for anyone's feelings.
But I kept moving, hamster-like, on a circular track,
Looking for elusive ways to begin healing, Pretending
to look forward, never looking back.

I spent my years, I thought, comfortably alone, Making
peace, making progress, making amends.
I may not be all the way home
But I can finally see where the road ends
And, perhaps, a way to finally atone.

So much sorrow, so much pain, and yet
There's still so much I'm longing to say,
So many bridges, so much water to forget,
You're the one I let slip away,
And you're the one I most regret.

No scrapbook pages, no love letters torn in half,
Not a single preserved moment from the past,
Or a faded, long-forgotten sepia-toned photograph.
This tragic, unrequited love, forever lost
Became, I fear, my final epitaph.

4
ON THE EDGE

I think I'm on the edge of something important.
I'm not certain, but I believe it may be true.
I'm standing on the precipice of something beautiful.
From my elevated perch I have a, breath-taking view.

Watching from this towering vantage point,
From this lofty perch, I'm able to see
A reverential vision of the landscape down below.
Elevation got the best of me.

Watch my hand shake;
Watch my heart break;
Watch me crying out in vain.
Nature's calling;
Rain is falling;
Won't you come and ease my pain?

I'm standing on the edge of fleeting moments,
Prepared to flip a coin and make a call.
I'm ready to take the plunge with you,
But I refuse to step up and take the fall.

I'm standing on the edge of a dangerous abyss,
Afraid of all the things I'm apt to see.
My acrophobia is nothing to dismiss,
Elevation got the best of me.

Watch my hand shake;
Watch my heart break;
Watch me crying out in vain.
Nature's calling;
Rain is falling;
Won't you come and ease my pain.

I'm standing, precariously on the edge
Between the dangerous and the divine,
And from this vantage point I'm able see
The razor-thin borderline.

I'm standing out here desperately hanging on.
Do I stay and fight or flee?
As the ground crumbles beneath my naked feet,
Elevation got the best of me.

Watch my hand shake;
Watch my heart break;
Watch me crying out in vain.
Nature's calling;
Rain is falling;
Won't you come and ease my pain?

"A poem is
what makes
you laugh, cry,
prickle, be silent,
makes your
toenails twinkle."

DYLAN THOMAS

5
THE RUSTY TALISMAN

The girl with honey hair and eye
Fools you with her churlish grin.
She wanders most days endlessly,
A childish regimen.

You don't know where you're headed
Because you don't know where you've been.
You're lost in your own footsteps,
No idea where to begin.

You say there are monsters in your closet,
But it's you that locked them in.
You've had every chance to release them,
Or make the choice to let them win.

They keep you awake and fearful,
And you appear disconsolate.
I'll help you learn to walk again
And leave with no regret.

The road you're apt to wander
Has a fork up ahead on the right.
I'll walk with you until you're there--
Someone to trust tonight.

Leave everything behind
Except your rusty talisman.
Keep your stony silence locked away,
And don't confess your sin.

There's ten thousand paths to wander,
Choose wisely and take care.
Only one will get you all the way home;
Count on me to get you there.

6
MISBEHAVED

The chilling tune, an ear worm,
Circled endlessly in my head,
And would not leave me alone.
Haunted me, hunted me
Beneath the stone
Where I hid.

It had a lyric, I'm certain,
Vague, simple, sad.
But the story, the rhyme are now gone,
The message and meaning disappeared.
Though I've forgotten every word
I can't forget the things we did.

There were games we played,
Writing our own rules,
A youthful masquerade.
We chased and ran and kicked the can,
And rolled and jumped and danced
And frequently disobeyed.

Don't tell us what to do,
Or choose the music we listen to,
Or the clothes we wear,
or the way we cut our hair.

The expectations were carefully arrayed,
But you'll recall the creative ways we misbehaved.

The course was clearly charted,
Everything in perfect order,
Orchestrated before we started.
The paths were mapped, marked, paved,
Until we went off-road, badly off course.
Of course, plans would have to be delayed.

This is the choice we willingly made,
The path we chose, the hidden trails we walked,
Uncharted mountains we crossed,
Rivers we had to ford, streams to wade.
The blisters on our feet
The price we gladly paid.

Our right to choose
Somehow went fundamentally wrong.
Nothing for the rebels, the wanderers,
The off-beat, off-road adventurers.
Rewards were reserved only for the valiant ones,
The followers, the obeyers, the strong.

When the sign said "stay out,
"To us it meant "come right in."
We were thrilled when we were right,
Delighted even more when we got it wrong.
Encouraged by those who rejected us
And said we don't belong.

When the public trial was held
In the court of one man's opinion,
Nerves were badly frayed
The media fawned,
the onlookers yawned
The jury hung and justice was again delayed.

There would never be a silver spoon,
Preferring only roads that forked,
Detours, closed doors, barricades,
Rust-worn voices that spoke
With honesty, promise-free, nothing guaranteed,
Revelations in the songs we played.

Still, we sought much higher ground,
No barrier, no railing,
A sharper turn, a steeper grade,

And the cliff would sometimes wash away.
Our choice: living on the edge
Was the price we gladly paid.

So we looked to the right
And then we left.
Grabbed a dull kitchen knife
And brazenly cut the cord.
It wasn't just freedom, rather courage,
That became our final reward.

"Modesty is a virtue not often found among poets, for almost every one of them thinks himself the greatest in the world"

MIGUEL DE CERVANTES

7
TOO LOUD TO SEE

Too loud to see,

Too dark to hear,

Too many shrill voices,

Too much anger,

Too much sorrow,

I fear.

Too many followers, too afraid to lead.

Lean on my strong arm,

I'll take it from here.

Too many excuses,

Everyone trying to please,

The medicines make it far worse

Than any disease.

Too many lyrics,

Not enough harmonies

To fill every need,

Your message of anger and hate

Can't possibly succeed.

Too many things to look at,

Not enough things to see.

Far too much double-talk,
Too many painted faces,
Their speech far to pedantic,
Lacking sincerity, angry, frantic.
Too many forked tongues, too much hypocrisy,
Too many self-appointed experts,
Persistent little gnats bothering me.

Too many facets,
Not enough facts,
Not enough contemplation,
There's a tendency to overreact.
Still so many crossroads,
Far too many semaphores,
Too many wandering souls
Getting nowhere because
They don't know what they're looking for.

Too many sightseers
Who fail to open their eyes,
Far too many hard edges,
No one willing to compromise
Everyone wants to move forward,
Reluctant to take the first step.
Be cautious, take care,
Let go of all your fears,
But hold on to your regrets.

Too many bridges yet to cross,
Too many boats left to burn,

Far too much impatience,
Far too many self-righteous speeches
Taken out of turn.
Is there anyone who can tell me, please,
As we cross the Rubicon,
How we'll ever make things right

By focusing only on the things that are wrong.

Too much ingratitude,
Never enough of giving thanks,
Too many judgements based
On money in the bank.
Too many ivory towers
--At least as far as I can see--
And if you don't like what is on the horizon,
Simply change the rules
And rewrite history.

Far too many people sleeping,
Far too many woke,
Far too many innocents
With a dagger in their cloak.
Still too much division, hate,

As we look for a brand-new start,
The more we try to pull together,
It seems,
The further we grow ap

8
UNCONDITIONALLY

It's hard to admit when I am weak,
When my heart goes one direction
And my brain the other way.
Lately I've been on a losing streak,
And couldn't avoid your careful inspection
With all my flaws on full display.

It's never been easy to admit my shame,
But your soulful gaze changed all the rules.
You saw right through my shallow veneer,
And I have never been the same
Since you pierced the veil of charlatans and fools,
And left the road map to forgiveness crystal clear.

Where did pain go?
How did you know?
When did you begin to love me so?
Why did you trust me?
How could I not seeThe tender romance
That has a penitent's hold on me?

I was so wrong;
You were so strong;
Now I know where I belong.
Why a second chance?

Did you know in advance
You'd forgive so willingly?
Why did you love me
And hold me so completely?
When did you begin to love me
Unconditionally?

There's a cavernous gap between my real intent
And actions that gave you so much pause.
I've been searching for a bridge that's safe to cross
To reassure you all the things I truly meant,
All my un-mended flaws,
Thoughtless words just so much dross.

So here is my best apology,
From one who is bruised and completely spent.
It comes from somewhere deep inside my wounded soul,
Foreign to my home-brewed theology,
But now on my knees, truly penitent.
Come help me close this painful, gaping hole.
Where did pain go?
How did you know?
When did you begin to love me so?

Why did you trust me?
How could I not see?
This tender romance
Has a penitent's hold on me?

I was so wrong;
You were so strong;
Now I know where I belong.

Why a second chance?
Did you know in advance
You'd forgive so willingly?
Why did you love me
And hold me so completely?
How do you keep loving me

Unconditionally?

9
WINTER'S BLUES

The birds are gone
And all the trees are bare,
The nights stretch on forever;
There's a knife of winter in the air.

Snow has settled secretly
On the roof tops in the Mews,
While sunsets paint the winter sky
In absolution hues.

The nights are cold and lonely;
The darkness calls, "beware."
Someone part the clouds,
There may be a sunset, somewhere, out there.

Winter stretches on forever
And stays far too long,
But the winter sunset palette
Paints a hopeful song.

Winter sun is orange and red;
Absent the greens and blues.
A winter sunset anxiously
Sends down its hints and cues.

Look to the west this evening–
There's redemption and good news:
A winter sunset is coming,
It's forgiving mercy long over due.

Winter is the pain of an icy heart;
The whispers you once knew;
But sunsets paint the winter sky
In absolution hues.

10
COMMAND Z

I've heard it said,
In song, speech, and on the street,
"The best things in life are free."
Who could argue with that?
Who could possibly disagree?

But I've been lately thinking
That of all the things there are
To do, and feel and see,
The very best thing in my life,
The best thing for me,
Resides in the far lower left corner
Of the computer keyboard,
The ultimate in forgiveness:
The simple touch of

Command Z.

Ah, The keyboard:
A writer's best friend, a writer's worst enemy.
It will take you to new places,
Or beat you senseless with alacrity.
The words I'm looking for come, slowly,

With malice, reluctantly.
Throw the whole page out, (or throw up.)

The writing belongs in the infirmary–
Better yet the morgue.
But there's an easy cure,
A writer's first choice, elemental,
Trustworthy and dependable,
Kind and non-judgmental.
Quick and easy,
The world's best editor:

Command Z.

Then all the awkward words,
Bad syntax, the clunky phrases
Are gone immediately, phew,
A close call, a chance for something new.
Like an old-fashioned eraser,
Vaporized all the sickly pages.
Far better, and more importantly
It takes you back in time,
Transports you, effortlessly,
Back to the beginning,
A start over, another take,
And how many times does that happen
For heaven's sake.
Peace, calm, and elusive serenity,

From the wise and clever **Command Z.**

And when my daily work is done,
I leave behind the writer's drudgery
And set out into the madding crowd,

Bouncing off the white-capped waves,
I look across the turbulent sea,

Bodies on top of bodies atop a watery grave.
A frightening mass of desperate faces,
The soulful flow and hum of humanity.
Among them are those that I have known,

Those who may have known me,A
nd I feign to look into their eyes,
Terrified of what I'll see.
I'm drowning out here,
No chance, I fear,

of a life jacket from Command Z.

As the waves pull me under,
Visions fill my eyes:
People I have cheated; times I have lied;
Some that I angrily chased away;
Abandoned, and left their dreams to die.
So much hope dashed, dispassionately,
So many things I neglected
Without remorse, without regret,

Without recourse, I shattered feelings effortlessly.
I shut out even closest friends,
Desperate for some privacy,
As if I'm the only one that matters,
A rock, an island in the sea.
Far, far away from my rescuer,

My last friend, Command Z.

Then the island is a prison,
Concrete, heavy iron bars,
Dungeons of regret, deep sorrow,
Painful bruises, deep scars,
Crocodiles below, lurking,
Swimming in a moat of misery,
I prepare to walk the green mile:
Death by electricity.

Then comes good news,
A change of plans, a change of heart,
For the wrongly accused, clemency.
"You have a clean slate," I am told.
"All transgressions expunged.
You are pardoned, you are free,
A stay of execution courtesy...
of Command Z."

Whether writing or fighting,
Winning or losing,
Hanging in or wearing out,
Learning or yearning,
Hurling words of hate, of help,
Living hopefully, or in a cloud of doubt,
Testing new forms of sincerity,
Or stuck in a rut of arrogance and vanity.

Bring all regrets to the altar,
Kneel, penitently.
Come seek the healing balm

With your mournful, soulful plea,
Raise a quiet finger,
The tender touch of a single key,
My trusted friend, My redeemer,

The humble Command Z.

It is my Pastor; my Priest; my Confessor;
My support group; my Shrink.
It is a best friend that nurtures me, encourages me
To move on and start over.
It is my chapter and verse,
It is my weekly sermon, my shaman,
It is my new age philosophy.
And in the end, it is this,

There in all its simplicity:
It is a mothers' kiss that makes everything better,
A warm embrace,
A bandage on your scraped knee,
A cookie and a glass of milk,
The maternal healing power,

The warm and loving arms of Command Z.

Count all the missed opportunities,
Turn around and look back
At the times you strayed and disobeyed,
And while Rome burned, you played
And became an emotional kleptomaniac,
Stealing from others what you thought you lacked,
Wallowing in self pity

And painted your whole world black,
Hit the wall and finally cracked.
Perhaps you haven't seen or heard
About the wizard's magic,
Right there in front of you
Where it's plain to see,
The last letter, the last key

The forgiving power of
Command Z.

"Poetry is the art of creating imaginary gardens with real toads."

MARIANNE MOORE

11
THE BOOK MARKER

You carry yourself with an aging grace,
Those lines that furrow your weathered face
Are markers of the passions you embraced,
Fleeting moments that may have gone to waste
Are there forever.

There's a burning ember behind your eyes,
A passion you cannot deny,
A futile effort if you try.
The sadness of a long goodbye
 Still flickers.

You hide behind your tempting grin,
Whether you lose the game or play to win,
Or chose to start all over again,
Open arms will welcome you in
With no regrets.

Every line that marks your weathered face
Are lines that wishing can't erase.
They're book markers to keep your place,
A gentle reminder just in case
You forgot the story.

There were friends who always stood by you,
And always found the good in you,
Pointed out what you should do,
Or hinted things may not be good for you,
And did them anyway.

Friends often fled from you,
Wounded hearts bled for you.
The painful things that were said about you
Brought out a darker dread in you,
But you survived.

Roads that were paved for you,
Crowds were well behaved for you,
Fighters saved by the bell for you,
Debts were counted and paid for you,
And all's forgiven.

Every line that marks your weathered face
Are lines that wishing can't erase.
They're book markers to keep your place,
A gentle reminder just in case
You forgot the story.

Countless tears were shed for you;
Heroes led the way for you,
And patiently walked ahead of you.
The hard things you never dared to do
Still haunt you.

Tall tales were sometimes told of you,
Spies came in from the cold for you,

Innumerable souls were bought and sold for you.
Heaven, clearly, broke the mold of you.
Believe it.

I told you I would always stay with you.
This is the promise that I made to you.
My plans were all best-laid for you,
Always tailor-made for you.
So keep on writing.

It's a tale of enemies and friends,
With no beginning, no end.
So, when the sun comes up again,
Remember stories of when
We had fences to mend,

Rules to bend,
Unwritten letters to send,
Promises to amend,
Expectations to upend,

Keep it real or just pretend,
You know where it all began.
Take up ink and pen,
Start writing your story again.
Every line that marks your weathered face,
Are lines that wishing can't erase.
They're book markers to keep your place,
A gentle reminder just in case
You forgot the story.

"Publishing
a volume of verse
is like dropping
a rose petal down
the Grand Canyon
and waiting
for the echo."

DON MARQUIS

12
THE CLOCKWORK UNIVERSE

Earth awakened this morning, refreshed
By the warm reception of its familiar guests,
Darkness for half of us, light for all the rest.
A planet renewed, yawned and stretched
Then resumed its precise axial turn.

Just enough spin to hold us on the ground,
Half the world hanging upside down,
Clinging effortlessly, without a sound,
Faith and hope have run aground
With still so much to learn.

A world that now has run amok,
Shattering the face of every clock,
As shepherds abandon helpless flocks,
Secrets in the vault, tightly locked
Away from curious eyes.

Pride and vanity, again are on the loose,
Led by the mob so maddeningly obtuse,
Left without a platform, no fans, no lectern, no excuse,
Forever changing the clockwork universe
And the rigidity we all despise.

All around, startling new levels of cowardice
Have led to an exuberant mass exodus.
Gather round, this is something no one wants to miss.
What sane person could possibly resist
This historic stampede.

Exactness is becoming a byword and a hiss,
A new approach to living, the masses now insist.
Facts and science readily dismissed
In favor of unsubstantiated verbal myths,
No arbiter to intercede.

Here comes the incidental paradox,
Rearranging natures building blocks,
The integration of the 13-hour clock,
Taking names and taking stock
Of all the changing attitudes.

Explained with a clever Venn diagram,
The argument of a polished flimflam man
Who couldn't pass the simple entrance exam,
Yet makes sense every now and then,
By accepting as truth, hollow, empty platitudes.

Rigidity is such a painful curse,
Ordering all integrity to disperse,
Feeling around your neck the hangman's noose
As the changing of the clockwork universe
Seems to have lost its rhythm.
Come, find peaceful calm and tranquility
Behind the concrete fence of anonymity,

Carefully avoiding any shade of enmity
From those who invoke populous banality.
Time to take a stand against, or march with them.

Logic strikes a dissonant chord,
Common sense grows increasingly absurdist,
Simple reason is traded for an earthly reward, And
wisdom is ordered to desist
Along the route of the collectivist parade.

The wolf pack still clinging to their pack of lies,
Deceit, seen as truth in someone else's eyes.
There will be no room for compromise
As wisdom weakens, then fades, then dies,
A reverent, whisper-quiet charade.

The strident new edges defined by the extreme,
Acceptable new science borders on obscene,
No latent fingerprints left at the scene, Rearranged
the way it might have been,
But highly contaminated.

Original thought is carried away in a funeral hearse,
In the tender care of a good night nurse.
Just when things couldn't seem worse
Came the death of the clockwork universe,
It's exactness highly overrated.

Read and re-read the same book, same woeful lines,
Memorize, regurgitate, leave originality behind,
Cancel the liturgy, cut the ties that bind,
Nothing left to change your mind,
Or accept a double-dog dare.

Folding laundry the proper way,
Vacuuming carpet, needlessly, three times a day,
No time to think, no time to get outside and play.
Following historic wagon ruts where they lay
Will get you absolutely nowhere.

Pick up the kids at half past three,
No one to argue with; no one will disagree,
No open debate; no conflict to referee,
Just a standard acquiescence is all there'll ever be.
Stand up, salute, and always say yes.

Three clocks in every room
Keep you precise, here, in your living tomb,
Never recognizing the dismal gloom
That crept in undetected behind the blood-red moon
You secretly detest.

Rise at dawn and punch the clock,
Get on the train with the rest of the flock,
Eight hours then crawl back under a rock,
No escape from this notorious prison block,
No windows, no light, no scenery.
Like a hamster in a cage
Fueling a silent, simmering rage,
Your biography is still unfinished and vague.
As your tragic story reaches its final page,

Close the cover, close the book, finis.
Stand here and recite chapter and verse
A memorized script carefully rehearsed,
Waiting for your trip in the long, black hearse,

Afraid to disrupt the clockwork universe
And chase a star or two.

Caught in the continuum of time and space,
Quoting science that fools can't ignore or replace,
Running blindly through the labyrinth at a deathly pace,
Erasing facts, putting rumors in their place
Is such a simple thing to do.

What a grand time to gather all the fools,
Twist and bend even tiny rules,
Each issued a full range of new tools
To tear down all the schools
And re-draw the narrow borderline.

Trying to reconnect space and time,
Recently acquitted of a senseless crime,
Walking a rocky road still largely undefined,
Who can make sense of this annoying pantomime?
Blind obedience suits you just fine.
Having to make fewer and fewer decisions,
Less bruising, less bleeding, fewer incisions,
Moving further away from heavenly visions,
Feeling comfortably at home with the precision
Of a clockwork universe.

In the darkest moments of a massive power outage,
We were all released from a fraudulent demurrage,
Delicately side-stepping disease-ridden sewage,
Never finding the breathless vigor of raw courage,
A self-administered spite.

Gone the disconsolate Sunday,
Abandonment, isolation the price you will pay
For allowing faith to get in the way
Of embracing machina mundi,
A more consistent source of light.

Five trillion planetary miles traversed,
Your mental expenses never fully reimbursed,
Your aching head under water, fully immersed
In the written confession, painfully coerced,
Your obeisance to the clockwork universe.

13
FOLLOWING CAIRNS

The road before me has far too many twists and turns,
And craggy, black lava boulders mark the way.
The air is gauzy thin, each breath a painful burn–
Not exactly what I had in mind today.
The old man of red-mountain seems bitter-cold and taciturn.
It's cowardly to turn around; too ominous to stay.

Following directions of every well-placed cairn,
Carefully pushing boulders straight up hill,
Missing, by just inches, the vital first and ten.
If you don't complete the trek right now, you likely never will.
So listen to the messages the pathway markers send,
Or remain a silent coward, inert and deathly still.

Relying on the ancient, mystic power of Zen
To show you footsteps, there, along the shore,
And taking stock it's meaning every now and then,
Strengthened, not weakened by the load you daily bore.
Difficult to know how, Impossible to know when,
Feeling as if you've somehow walked this trail before.

Ancient footsteps just below, whisper a plaintive call,
Ignored, forgotten, and daily desecrated,
Where flash-flood torrents carved the canyon walls
And left the riparian floor wounded, decimated,
Leaving jagged edges that portend a tragic fall,
Only to see it, in time, renewed, revived, and re-created.

Step cautiously, and leave your alms,
Follow carefully the cairn-marked trail.
Touch, feel, embrace the ancient healing balm,
Wash clean your burdens and trials;
And breathe in the peaceful, forgiving calm,
As you walk these unforgiving, torturous miles.

Feel it, live it, until, at last, you return.
Remember every rugged peak; every stream you had to
ford, Hear again the echoes of the secrets you learned;
The wisdom of the canyons safely stored,
Preserved in a red-clay, Anasazi urn,
Faith in humanity, at last restored.

You've banished the invading Mongol hordes
To a point of no return,
Dismissed all pretentious overlords,
And every bridge has burned.
Death by invective, not the sword,
A slow, shameful retreat back to Karakorum

14
NOTHING MUCH WRONG

I don't think any one ever had heartburn
When I turned and walked away.
I don't recall that there was anyone
Who ever begged me to stay

No broken hearts to sing about;
No shattered dreams to make a song;
There were times when nothing seemed quite right,
But nothing seemed fatefully wrong.

How can there ever be a poet
Who can't write a decent rhyme?
How can there be a ballad
When no one is charged with a crime.

I can't think of a single person
Who ever bid me a fond farewell,
Or listened when I came home from the sea
With painful stories to tell.

There's no one standing on the dock,
No one come to bid me adieu.
No one to send me a dear-john letter,
Or promising "I'll be right here when you're through."
How can there ever be a poet
Who hasn't got a clue?

How can there be a soulful lament
Without a heartbreak or two?

No one ever stood as a witness,
No one ever put me through hell,
No lover ever watched my train pull away,
Or bailed me from a cell.

It's a rotten life to have been so good,
It's been a terrible twist of fate,
I never faced a firing squad,
No stay of execution ever came too late.

How can there ever be a writer
Who can't spill pain onto the page?
How can there be a memorable tune
Without jealousy, anger or rage.

I've got no sorrows to sing about,
Never needed to have a fresh start,
No big regrets to think about,
No apologies, no broken heart.

What a horrible thing to have lived with;
It's been a terrible burden to bear--
To have just one woman always at my side;
One lover, patiently standing there.

I can't write a song when there's nothing much wrong.
And I can't find the tunes or the rhyme.
But if I had to chose one woman,
Just one single woman,
I'd do it again every time.

15
THE FOUNTAIN OF DOUBT

Pull your chair up close to me,
Where I can look into your eyes.
I have some bad news to share.
I doubt you'll be surprised.

It's best for us to part for a while;
I hope you will agree.
There were many times I tried to walk away,
But your heart had a firm grip on me.

> *Listen to this:*
> *It's a raging silence that you hear.*
> *It's the shadow of doubt*
> *I've been thinking about,*
> *Quiet and painfully clear.*

It hasn't been an easy thing to stay,
And walk your narrow, one-way street.
But there are so many places yet to explore;
So many people to meet.

I'm not really going far away,
And I haven't mapped out the route.
But I'm going to lay down new footprints,
And drink from the fountain of doubt.

Listen to this:
It's a thunderous silence that you hear.
It's the shroud of doubt
I've been talking about,
Quiet and crystal clear.

All those times when you and I
Survived on trust and certainty,
All the black and white noise we heard,
Were someone else's naiveté.

Be angry with me, resent me, despise me,
But it's still time for me to leave.
Please don't judge me too hastily,
Believe what you must believe.

Listen carefully to this:
It's the painful silence that you hear.
It's the reasonable doubt
I've been talking about,
Quiet and crystal clear.

It will come as a massive blow to you--
The voices I now can hear--
But I've won the self-loathing battle,
And silenced my innocent fear.

So it's best for us to part for a while;
Walk away and clear our minds,
Wander and soften hard edges;
Who knows what we may find.

Listen to this:
It's a rumble of silence you hear.
It's the simplest kind of doubt
I've told you about,
Quiet but deafeningly clear.

So it's best for us to part for a while,
Walk away and clear our minds.
To wander off and soften hard edges,
And find truths of a different kind.

I'm not really going far away,
And I haven't mapped out the route.
But I'm going to lay down new footprints,
And, for a time, drink from the fountain of doubt.

16
THE ROAD TO NOWHERE

There's a passageway that takes me
Close to you, yet often far removed.
At times it drops me close to your side,
Depending on its mood.

I can travel on wings to mountaintops,
And, at other times, down to lowly places.
I'm sure I've seen more highs than lows,
And pain on countless faces.

There's a long, long road I've travelled,
As far away as a man can get.
A ten thousand-mile roadshow,
With stretches I'd much rather forget.

Take me far away from here;
Take me away from everything I've ever feared.
Take me to the sacred water;
Let me hear the counsel of the grand vizier.

There's a long, long stretch of nothing,
Just outside of dead and gone.
The warning signs are telling me
"That it's time to move along."

The road takes a sharp right turn
Just before the town of Hopelessness,

Then cuts through Abandon All Hope,
As the road stretches north by northwest.

Take me far, far away from here;
Take me away from everything I've ever feared.
Take me to the sacred water,
Let me hear the voice of the grand vizier.

The motor's tuned and running smooth,
And ready for the street.
Something just blew in on the wind
That says "Time to move your feet."

There's a rainstorm over Denver,
And snow up on the great divide,
It's tough to cross the desert west,
But I'll let you decide.

Take me far away from here,
Take me away from everything I've ever feared.
Take me to the sacred water,
Let me learn at the feet of the grand vizier.

Put me back on the lonely road,
That runs through Here and Now.
There's no compass, map, or GPS,
But I'll still find you somehow.

Take me far, far away from roads
That lead, in time, nowhere,
Take me to the healing waters,
Let me find you when I get there.

"**POETRY** is when an emotion has found its thought, and the thought has found words."

ROBERT FROST

17
MY IDENTITY

My identity is gone, taken.
Someone broke in and stole it with a hack.
I want to reclaim my life,
I want to go home and get it back.
My feet won't move, no moving forward,
I'm stagnating, evolving no more,
Damned to a life of failure,
Stuck in the eternal revolving door.

Bring on the tribulation,
I can probably handle another heap.
Pour it on, dump it out, bring a truckload,
Misery, it appears, is cheap.
Plan your assault on me,
It matters very little
If you attack from the front
Or meet me somewhere in the middle.

I've been badly beaten by the elite ruling class
With their toys and playgrounds and rapacious trysts,
While I faced every day with failure, and falls,
Disastrous, unpredictable turns and twists.
Punch the clock, pull the lever
No escape they insist,
Banished to the bottom
Of the dank, slimy abyss.

I punched the clock robotically,
Lined up, collected my wages
And kept a record of nickels and dimes,
Human tragedy on brittle pages.
Ruled by rule of indiscriminate law,
Haunted by a phalanx of cruel men
Who presided at the factory gate,
I resolved to never be made a fool again.

But with a contract signed in blood
I got stuck in the rusted turnstile
"Relax," the foreman said to me,
"You're going to be here for a while.
You approved a no escape clause
When you signed the Devil's pact.
You have been scammed again
As a matter of fact."

Line up, shut up, comply, conform,
Forty-five years in a hard-labor prison
As a clock puncher, clock watcher,
With no appeal, it's the final decision.
I was cheated, mistreated,
Along with the masses, complainers, and moaners,
But there'll be no reparations
From the slavery owners.

Just as you are ready to fly,
Check your boarding pass,
You've been bumped to the back of the line
Just behind the hoarding class.

Glorious conquests were yours for the asking,
Just for you, anonymous you,
The back-pocket flask king,
The empty bottle is nothing new.

18
FOGGY BOTTOM

I pass by the gates of Langley each day
And try to guess what goes on inside.
It's a bulwark of freedom and democracy--
But the ten-foot fence is electrified.

A regiment has fallen from the skies--
All manner of peering and padded feet.
An air drop of snoopers, spooks and spies,
And privacy is in retreat.

I've pried and tried a thousand times
But, still, there is nothing to see;
Still not a single thing to see
Within the gates of Langley.

Oh come, oh come all you beltway bandits,
Come and cross the bridge with me.
Let me show you all the monuments
Built to the pirates of D.C.
Find a spot 'neath the shade of the cherry trees,
Enjoy the stunning view,
But leave the back door open because
The constitution may not be a good fit for you.

A phalanx of dubious confidants
Follow rules not written in the books,
Who know exactly what they want, we're told,
But not a clue about where to look.

And here comes the mighty K street brigade,
In lock-step, and monogrammed sleeves,
Tromping through the fields of Foggy Bottom,
Alan Edmonds filled with mud and sleaze.

The secrets will remain invisible;
Nothing there for you and me.
Nothing of worth for you and me
Inside the gates of Langley.

Oh come, oh come you beltway bandits,
Come and cross the bridge with me.
Let me show you all the monuments
Built to the pirates of D.C.
Find a spot 'neath the shade of the cherry trees,
Enjoy the stunning view,
But leave the back door open because
The constitution may not be a good fit for you.

They cover their ears and cover their eyes
And fortify the wall of pretense.
They cross the river at Rochambeau
To proclaim a beltway innocence.

They're fully funded, fully armed,
Through the swamps, in four/four time,
They march blindly to Pretoria--
All on someone else's dime.

I'm looking for an honest man,
Here in the land of the free,
To come and drink a pint with me
Outside the gates of Langley.

Oh come, oh come you beltway bandits,
Come and cross the bridge with me.
Let me show you all the monuments
Built to the pirates of D.C.
Find a spot 'neath the shade of the cherry trees--
Enjoy the stunning view,
But leave the back door open because
The constitution may not be a good fit for you.

I'm standing, still standing
Waiting patiently
For just the right communiqué
Outside the gates of Langley.
Outside the gates of Langley.
The lonely voice of democracy,
Standing patiently,
Waiting vainly
Outside the gates of Langley.

"POETRY is the synthesis of hyacinths and biscuits."

CARL SANDBERG

19
THE TYRANTS OF THE HABOOBS

There's a summer wind
Blowing just outside my door—
A calm, welcome breeze,
Nothing more,
Leaving everyone, mostly, in peace,
And comfortably at ease.
Just now, a peaceful zephyr
Zipping through the branches,
Quietly shaking the leaves--
A million independent dances.
And in an instant
It begins to howl, then roar;
Then scream,
Rattling the windows
And kicking in the door.
This is something I've seen
So many times before,
And here it is again—
The caprice,
The uncertainty
Of the desolation wind.

I've been robbed and cheated
And battered so completely;
I've often been defeated,
My life completely shattered,
And all my dreams scattered,
By a malevolent, unremitting wind.
I've been badly beaten and broken
By the force of the gale,
And so many curses unspoken.
My good name has been badly abused;
Now here I stand accused
Of some unconfessed sin,
Before the judgment bar
Of the desolation wind.

"You will travel the way the wind blows--
This is what justice demands."
Where it takes you no one knows,
And even fewer understand.
It's a dark and cruel fate
That dries up the land,
Turns fertile soil into sand,
And with an iron fist,
Seizes the upper hand,
And deals you a stern warning,
A harsh reprimand,
Then sends you on your way.
Where it leads you, no one is certain,

No one can really say.

Because no one really knows,

Hour by painful hour,

Which way the wind blows—

Except that now

It's time to hit the road,

Time to go,

Despite the heavy load.

I put my cap on tight—

Down around my ears--

Even the North Star is hidden and out of sight;

Nothing to rely on,

No one to calm my fears.

Darkened, desolate, and dim,

These are the orders from the judge and jury,

Ominous, grim,

A final decree

From the desolation wind.

Out in the wasteland,

Now completely alone,

I begin to see the power it has shown,

The path of destruction left behind,

The evil temperament,

Blindly, brutally, unkind.

Unhealed wounds agape,

No alternatives, no escape

From the wind that leaves the earth

Scorched and bare,

And brings mountains down,
Completely at will,
As if there was never anything there.
It carelessly carves canyons and walls,
Wantonly covering the arid desert
With its favorite gusts,
It's swirls, and squalls;
Moves the sand and leaves behind only stones;
Don't beg for forgiveness;
Don't come looking to atone.
It's a harsh master--
Too fickle to face on your own.
You're playing a game you can never win,
You must learn the rules,
And accept the cruelty of
The desolation wind.

My face is tough as leather;
Hands as strong and rough as stone;
The wind peels off it's last, thin, layer,
Leaving only bone.
The wind is all I've ever known,
Everywhere I've come from,
And all the places I have been.
Don't get too comfortable--
You may have to pack your bags again
And go in the direction it sends you—
A new journey about to begin--
The arbitrary decree of
 That desolation wind.

It comes in a variety of shapes and sizes
And hums a dozen different tunes:
The hurricane, the typhoon,
And we give them human names
So we have someone on whom to place the blame.
The tropical storm; the trades;
The tornadoes; hurricanes;
The sirocco;
The ones you've already seen
And a few you didn't know;
And in the end
The results are always the same:
Pick up the pieces,
File a claim, endure the pain.
The tumult left you outside looking in,
Ravaged by the forces,
Controlled by the unbridled power
Of the desolation wind.

It will leave you decimated;
High and dry;
Shredded to little pieces;
Worse than we anticipated.
And then it will leave you,
And forget you, by and by.
This is the wind's lament,
This is the intent:
To leave you baffled, confused, mystified--
How quickly it came and went--

And left the whole world
Broken and terrified.
In an instant, twisted and bent;
It's a treacherous game
And you can never win;
Chances are very slim
That this is the last time you'll witness,
The terror of the desolation wind.

There's a restlessness,
A relentlessness,
Full of rancor and hate,
That the wind brings along
Following in its wake.
It's a constant, painful blowing,
Without ever knowing
The whys and the hows,
Only the here's and now's,
And the very bad news
That there is another storm waiting—
Lined up in the queue,
Nothing much to do
Because it's a personal wind--
Aimed straight at you.
But there's nothing left to fear.
And you've learned how to react
To the changing moods,
Of the the coward.

The tyrant of the Haboobs,
The mercenary, the fickle whims,
The unforgiving torture of
The desolation wind.

Blow then you wretched wind,
Roar away if you must.
You're bringing with you
A welcome rainstorm I trust.
Be wicked, be fierce,
Take your best shot,
You'll soon end up
Just another storm we all forgot.
We may not be able to stop it,
We may not be ready for yet another fight,
But the calm is coming—
The calm always follows the darkest night—
Be ready when the howling horrors begin,
Be assured it will come again,
The patterns of the weather are absolute.
Stand firm, stand resolute,
Set your feet,
Be strong, lean in.
You are still the master of
The desolation wind.
The winds and the waves shall obey His will;
Peace, peace be still.

20
A RAVEN'S SCREECH

Welcome to the new America
Where every person seems to have taken a seat
On the extreme left,
Or the hard-core right,
In a windowless room
Devoid of light.
Armed with polished swords, gleaming edges,
Lonely one-man battlefields,
Hanging from rocky cliffs,
Dangling from roof-top ledges—
America's desperation,
This generational plight
Where everyone is focused on being right,
Instead of working together
To get it right.

It's an all-night, endless quarrel,
Shrill voices, a raven's screech,
Angry vitriol spewing
From hollow speeches
Telling us where we've gone wrong
Instead of time spent—
Far more wisely—
Just trying to get along.

Silver bullets flying
In an endless war of words,
The lofty, the arrogant,
The angry, the absurd.
Listen to yourself, brother against brother,
With little chance of compromise,
A sentence of death
To anyone who even tries.

Come see the new Colossus,
Come bear witness at the altar of extremes
Where old glory still flies,
Badly worn, tattered, frayed
And pulling apart at the seams.
Stars and stripes above a sea of demagogues,
Nothing even vaguely reminiscent
Of one nation under God.
Neighbor against neighbor,
A street brawl,
A petty quarrel,
Proving who is right and who is wrong,
Too busy fighting
Instead of tearing down walls
And finding ways to get along,
Midst a stream of abrasive noise,
The endless tossing of bricks and bats,
When it's so easy to love your neighbor—
Could we, at the very least,
Try that?

"POETS aren't very useful because they aren't *consumeful* or very *produceful*."

OGDEN NASH

21
THE HUMAN ZOO

I've circumnavigated the globe,
Guided only by arrogance and the stars,
And a wanderlust gone awry.
Not much to think about,
Nothing much to write home about,
No one at the other end standing by.

I visited the king and queen,
And had a deep discussion
With a third-world president.
I've seen the gallery of snobbery,
Victims of their robbery,
And the revolutionary spirit they foment.

I've dined with senators and judges,
And those who count the beans,
Cautiously moving the decimals
To make the numbers come out right--
The numbers never seem just right--
To the insider who buys and sells.

There were teachers who spoke with reverence,
Professors who spoke in tongues,
And a voice so strangely reminiscent.
Listen carefully to what they say,
The facts may yet be on their way,

Wrapped in a deeper form of entitlement.
I've dined at length with moneymen;
Partied long and hard with funny men,
And those of the laugh-challenged league.
They could quote all the beatitudes,
But deferred to worn out platitudes
For the victims of their charitable fatigue.

I've climbed an unknown mountain,
To find the wise man of the rocks,
Who dabbles in the existential.
But he struggles to be exact,
Wisdom, of course, is never exact,
At the very best, it's all coincidental.

I've befriended preachers and vagabonds,
Romantics, painters, poets,
And writers obliquely oppressed.
I've forged some lasting friendships,
Ruined one half of all my friendships,
And offended all the rest.

Here comes the carnival,
Rolling in to town.
It's never quite what you expect.
But still they put on a show—
Man can they put on a show.
The price of admission: your fealty and respect.

Stand up, sit down,
Salute, stand mute and bow
To the icons of ineptitude.

You give and they take,
And they take and take some more,
And demand that you show a little gratitude.

And then there is the matter
Of planned, incompetent looting,
And a calculated embezzlement.
It's gathering interest on the debt--
There will always be enormous debt--
And always organized, radical dissent.

"Come one and all," cries the barker,
To see the carnival side show,
And all the freaks you'd expect.
Lay down all your money--
They always want your money--
But never ask for your respect.

It's a cage, perhaps a prison,
Depending on your point of view.
The "guests" are locked alone in solitaire.
Don't feed the animals,
It's dangerous to feed the animals,
Keep walking and try not to stare.
The creatures are all roar, no bite.

Nothing much to their rehearsed dance,
Or their uneasy, pacing back and forth,
With no plan for the big escape--
Pray they never escape--
Before you get you money's worth.

An outrageous point of view,
And unreasonable demands,
Are the things you expect to find
In the search for buried treasure—
There is no buried treasure—
Only truth of a distant kind.

It's a grand day for an outing.
Come and be enlightened
If you've nothing better to do.
See the faces behind the bars,
See the defrocked movie stars,
Just another fine day at the human zoo.

22
THE APOTHECARY JAR

Turn on the art deco Crosley
But wait for the tubes to glow.
You'll need an outlet but not an antenna,
But that's something you may already know.
Let the static crackle, and listen carefully to what is said,
And tune in your favorite old radio show.
Try not to laugh or take sides with the mourners,
Celebrate liberation instead
As you lose your self in the lonely corners
Of your tragic and empty king size, antique bed.

We sat on the concrete walls on the corner
By the abandoned Sears Roebuck store,
With some of the righteous and some of the mourners,
And a large crowd of faces we'd never seen before,
Eating Mexican tacos and other things of curious debate.
When the governor's henchmen stopped by for a reprieve
They had been warned that it was far too late,
At the food truck everyone knows,
Finding only crumbs and warm orange Jarito
And nowhere else they needed to go.

One too many hats in the ring,
Not enough meat to go around,

And not enough laments for the mourners to sing.
It was agreed we would have to lower the bar,
Though that would leave the vultures circling,
We knew the secrets couldn't get very far,
Stored in the antique apothecary jar
On the top shelf behind the green depression glass
And the cobweb-strewn rule books
Meant only for the elite ruling class.

Wednesdays at the corner food truck,
Surrounded by undeserving celebrants
Who had finally run out of adoration and luck,
Joined us there on the corner
With the singers and dancers and downtown debutants,
The assessors, the professors, and second-guessers,
The ass-kissers, the mourners, and the dilettantes
Who were down to their very last buck.
They didn't know the difference between needs and wants
So they took an entirely different stance.

The gold leaf invites of the elite
Were of no value at the corner taco stand
Where on the street, we eat with hands.
They have come to post their unreasonable demands.
All efforts failed to keep them at bay.
They paid off the unofficial door-keepers
As they broke down all the doors--
A game the elite always play--
And came right in, with their trail of effluvium
And logic that left us hollow and numb.

The tragically desperate crumb lickers
Were too late to renegotiate the hoax,
So, they stormed the palace without tickets
And swam across piranha infested motes.
The mourners seemed so humble and earnest,
Hiding with their daggers and cloaks,
As they warily poked at the hornet's nest,
No one cried, no one murmured, no one spoke.
No crumbs were left for all the rest,
And the kangaroo court became a joke.

Destroyed by the double-bladed axe,
Everyone forgot to play by the rules,
And suddenly couldn't remember the facts
Established by the mourners, the foot soldiers, the fools.
Possessed of a wanton disregard,
They mounted a full-force frontal attack
Carrying signs saying, "Not in my back yard."
And with a blatant tampering of the jury,
 You may, in the end, rightly ask
"What, me worry?"

The blistering pace that we set
At the very least made for good ink.
But the lofty goals were mostly unmet,
And fallout was not what you would think.
The mourners set a table for two,
Oblivious to the lingering threat,
Cluelessly dined on a bland, meatless stew--

A folly, we believed, they would come to regret.
There was so little left for us to do
Except, next time, cast a wider net.

When you're defeated and emotionally spent,
And your suspenders are a little too tight,
Simply stop paying the exorbitant rent
And declare that you won the fight.
Go cry on the shoulder of entitlement,
Or listen to the sermon of mortal men—
A worthy substitute for diazepam.
A promising new initiative
That sounded so good on paper
Left the mourners drained, with nothing to give.

So, let's all plan to meet on the corner
At the food truck everyone knows.
Now that you have become one of the mourners,
Come, and I'll buy you a plate of street tacos,
Some fresh carne asada,
And a heaping portion of crow.
The food truck may leave—the end of the show—
Just like your fifteen minutes of fame,
So, let's raise a cold bottle of orange Jarito
And get back in the miserable game.

23
WAXEN WINGS

The invitation just arrived--
Silver ink, embossed.
There was no security to bribe,
But, at what price, the social cost?

It's got the right name, date and place--
Looks like a haughty crowd.
I'm just a name without a face,
No one like me is ever allowed.

Send regrets or an RSVP?
To insult or to appease?
To be seen or just to see?
Black tie only, if you please.
Bravely step outside your home,

You lonely misanthrope.
All the decadent people will come,
So don't abandon hope.

The last soiree touched a painful nerve,
An emotionally high price to pay.
The bon vivants lost their collective verve,
And vultures circled their wary prey.

Morning, indeed, did come again,
And so too regret and pity.
The in-crowd now is not so in,
Nor the aging, the handsome, the pretty.

There rose, that day, a different shade of dawn,
A paler, softer, incandescent light.
The respectable crowd had come and gone,
To your relief and your great delight.

There were footprints in the cool, wet sand,
Beside the dry-docked boats;
The socialites had all been banned
From sowing conspicuous wild oats.

So many ashen faces,
All the popular cliques had split,
Offering to gladly trade places,
But the glass slipper wouldn't fit.

Across the gangplank to the ship;
They set sail for ports unknown.
The cool, the trendy, the hip,
And all the free-birds had flown.

Fly away Jack, fly away Jill
Don't get too close to the sun.
You've got a different plan and always will,
Until your waxen wings come undone.

Let the updrafts carry you higher,
Don't get too close to the sun,
Keep chasing every noble desire
Until your final race is won.

No need to be so isolated,
You lonely misanthrope.
Your CV needs to be updated,
As you walk the social climber's tight rope.

24
MISSING PIECES OF THE PUZZLE

I tried my best to solve it,
But got it mostly wrong.
It was such a complex puzzle
With a couple of pieces gone.
It's still unfinished,
There on the table,
And I would gladly put it away,
Find the missing pieces and be done
If only I were able.

The pieces are all the same shape,
In muted shades of gray.
No cozy cabin in the glen,
No colorful garden bouquet.
Without any straight edges,
It's a chaotic, fools' game,
No corners, no beginning, no end--
The torment of the jigsaw--
A fiendish and tiresome shame.

And then there are your eyes,

A never-ending puzzle when I stare.

No enmity, no tenderness, no anger,

So very little of anything inside there.

A dense fog, a chilling morning mist,

Cast in a dull, murky gray,

Neither shallow nor endlessly deep,

What do you see? What do you feel?

Your eyes give nothing away.

Then there is your voice, your song,

Harsh, brittle, a coarse sandpaper grit,

The painful lyrics are forgettable

And I can't make sense of it.

No melody, no chorus, no memorable hook,

Just three notes, all of them sung off key.

A repetition, no chorus, no second verse

No searing emotion from the heart,

This abrasive scream, a puzzle to me.

But, it's a puzzle for someone else to solve,

Someone else's table, some other day.

I'm done, finished with the beast,

Put it on a shelf, very high, very far away,

Somewhere I can't see it, out of sight, out of reach,

Where I can't hear it call my name,

"Come back you coward,"

Don't give up and walk away:

An unfinished puzzle my personal bane.

And here you lie beside me,
Your finished picture still unclear.
You're a thousand different pieces
Minus one or two, I fear.
You'll remain unfinished, unsolved, for a time,
Your colors are a soft, muted hue,
Your edges impossible to define,
Your vagaries, your uncertainties
Won't let me see it through.

"You will find poetry nowhere unless you bring some of it with you."

JOSEPH JOUBERT

25
TRUTH ON TRIAL

The trial of the blonde actress we all knew,
Began early that spring.
Her appearance was long overdue,
Outlandish accusations flew,
And truth was granted a change of venue.

Typecast as the femme fatale
On the pages of the supermarket rags,
She was once the belle of the ball,
Now armed with lawyers and gall,
Truth missed the open casting call.

Recall the night of the incident--
Darkness at the scene of the crime.
The case seemed flawed and inconsistent,
But the D.A. wouldn't relent,
And truth, conveniently, came and went.

No real evidence was ever found,
But who cares, in an orange-neon court.
As the complex case unwound,
The facts in the case were mostly banned,
And truth was nowhere to be found.

The trial of the century was much ballyhooed,
As questioning finally began.
She was famous and everyone already knew

She was no paragon of virtue,
So the truth came in dull, grayish hues.

She thought she could beat the polygraph,
And volunteered to give it a try.
The paparazzi snapped ten thousand photographs,
As she was writing her headstone epitaph,
And truth, now a punchline, seemed to get the last laugh.

The inspector's team was undermanned,
And the evidence was visibly thin.
The barristers unleashed their demands,
On everyone who took the stand,
And all agreed to let the truth be damned.

The crowds came in boats, trains, and busses,
And the media hoards took control.
They proclaimed, "you must trust us",
But if this is true justice,
It'll never work for the rest of us.

Everyone turned to watch the brash, young D.A.,
As he dramatically pointed to the blonde.
Her head, in advance, served up on a tray,
"To the gas chamber without delay."
It was truth on trial that day.

He always gets the conviction,
This relentless Judas of the judiciary.
He beats witnesses into submission,
Falsehoods become his addiction,
And truth comes with myriad pre-conditions.

The artist sketched the dangerous blonde,
As the facts began to unfold.
Her Hollywood face was ashen and drawn,
Decorum and civility both completely gone,
And truth would face the firing squad at dawn.

Moment by moment the plot changed,
As the witnesses forgot memorized scripts.
Every time the gavel banged,
The demagogues had another harangue,
But it was truth that was ultimately hanged.

The star witness made a frank admission
About his role in the crime.
But he confused fact with fiction,
And mixed reality with supposition.
Truth, in the end, escaped extradition.

New evidence was conveniently created,
By the boys in their robes and curly wigs.
Hopes for acquittal faded,
When dignity and fairness abated,
And the truth was what anyone made it.

The jury was sent to deliberate
With a stern caution from the bench.
The blonde tried to guess her fate,
While the crowds spewed venom and hate,
And truth, in the end, came far too late.

When the final gavel sounded,
A dull wooden thud from on high,

The juror's votes were all counted,
"Hang her," the crowd all demanded,
And a new form of justice was branded.

The news, at last, proclaimed the decision,
That the truth would be locked up for life.
Under the spotlight of erudition,
As the facts gave way to expedient ambition,
Truth and justice had its final benediction.

26
VOICE OF A TROUBADOUR

Who gives permission to write a song?
Who decides when the lyrics are just right,
Or when the melody turns out wrong?
Who will referee the fight?
Who can know where awkward notes don't belong?
They sounded good late last night.
Have courage now, believe in yourself, be strong,
And get ready for the music revolution you'll incite.
Your instincts, it turns out, were right all along,
Out of shadows, but still too frightened by the light,
It's your time, something you simply cannot prolong:
You've captured the voice of the quietly emerging zeitgeist.

It's the weary, well-seasoned voice of a troubadour,
Well-known, well-loved, well-worn,
Stuck in a slow moving, revolving door,
A comfort, a muse, a confidant, a thorn,
Writing metaphors no one's ever heard before
And uncovering a lost genre, newly reborn.
Lyrics purchased from the second hand store,
Pages shredded, burned, cast away, torn,
Rhyming patterns too hard to explain, harder to ignore,
Weather-beaten, road-weary, emotionally drained, forlorn,
And a passionate fan base-- lunacy to the core--
Leaving you exposed, wasted, cut, and neatly shorn.

You shared uncomplicated, written phrases
That, once, seemed vaguely prophetic,
Coming, cautiously in measured phases
Now a bit tired and overly dramatic.
You can still feel the etched lines on tear-stained faces–
Monochromatic Venetian masks–painful and wantonly tragic.
There are too many insults you simply cannot erase,
By invoking voodoo curses and strange magic.
A cowardly figure hiding behind curtains of lace,
The sad tale boring and painfully anticlimactic.
In a final burst of passion, largely gone to waste,
Time to turn off the light and snuff out the final candlewick.

Remember your feeble, first attempts at poetry–
A quick reminder that nothing is built to last–
The insightful lyrics that still haunt me,
Conjuring up relics of our ancient past.
They opened my eyes and helped me see
Heartbreaks of the working class,
A chaotic, uncontrollable volatility
With armies invading record stores en masse
To hear the pain of your emotional poverty.
On the stage, confident and unabashed,
When your overwrought philosophy
Wilts and fades beneath the unforgiving lash.

Some melodies are impossible to kill,
Lyrics full of half-truths cleverly denied,
A haunting voice that lingers still,
A flame that long, long ago died.

Prisoners have been taken against their will,
Inner-longings quick to bury, quick to hide.
Sticky fingers in an empty till,
A dearth of humility, an overabundance of pride,
Believing that no one else would ever fill the bill.
Changing minds, changing styles, and turning tides.
Conjuring emotions that are hard to kill
When passion, art, and profit collide.

Scored and sung in a rhapsodic way,
The tunes that always feel just right,
The perfect melody can never be taken away
From empty beds and endless dark nights,
From lovers who have wandered aimlessly away,
From those too exhausted to fight,
A true romance carelessly tossed away.
The quatrain that's meant to assuage or incite,
A clever poet by day
And a cunning thief by night.
Bury your pain, hide it safely away,
While the music publicly depicts your tragic plight.

Crafted by mortals but clearly heaven sent,
With a clean slate and ample leeway,
Capturing dismay, singing of discontent
The joyful chorus of the cabaret
Began to sing, free-versing as they went,
As if molding a softened block of clay.
Spewing from the list of legally approved compliments,
A split personality on a divided highway,

Counting consonants, crossing continents,
Preparing for take-off, paused on the runway.
After all, it's just another catchy pop song experiment,
Not a four-hour passion play.

Go back to the very beginning
When harsh realities first came in to play.
Crueler times, ruthless and often unforgiving,
Which rules to reject, a very short list to disobey,
Years of rejection, dismay, starving, barely living.
Plunging headlong into the convoluted music fray,
Theorizing, baptizing, keep the faith, keep on believing.
Fingers bleeding, scraping by day to day,
Abandoned all values for a complete reimagining.
Who's next on the list for me to betray?
Living on pride and well-honed skills at flattering,
Who and where is my next prey?

Tragically felled by the climactic final chorus,
Listening for clues in the faraway lament,
You took it all, leaving nothing for the rest of us
As admiration and adulation came and went.
Manufacturing reasonable industry success,
Boundaries yet to cross; rules to circumvent,
Your voice once preternaturally sonorous,
Skipped town to avoid a certain indictment,
But kept your whereabouts strictly hush-hush,
Yielding to the entreaties of the tenacious serpent
Whose intrepid disciples came between us
And left us ripped apart and publicly penitent.

What a tragedy, the unrehearsed farewell show
On a remote stage, singing and picking your final outro.
Fame and fortune came and went,
A standing ovation your final sacrament.
The peripatetic country preacher,
Believing you can still reach her
With lyrics that are badly out of style,
Melodies summoned, in absentia, to a trial
Where only the gallows await.
Guilty of forgery, phoniness and hate,
A comeback, coming far to late,
Unrelenting regrets your final fate.

27
THE STEALTH OF ZAO

Aurora Borealis draped its icy hues,
And danced to the music it knew.
Your inept approbation
Disrupted the illumination,
From your well-worn, antique, rustic pew.

You spent most of your life digging,
To understand the end from the beginning.
Nothing is what you expected,
Your theories ineffective,
And lights along the shore are quickly dimming.

You're in the fight,
You're in the race,
You've set the winning pace.
Don't let them see your doubt,
Pain is what it's all about
Until it's over.

Caught in the flames of the inferno,
How could you possibly know?
They taught with the all the usual tropes,
And extinguished every flicker of hope,
And doubt landed a staggering blow.

Dawn arrived, the orange glow of Zao,
True humility followed somehow.
The quiet whispers of the shaman,
Revealed we had nothing in common,
While you painfully broke a sacred vow.

You're in the fight,
You're in the race,
You've set the winning pace.
Don't let them see your doubt,
Suffering is what it's all about,
Until it's over.

The halo you wore so long ago
Is dimming and has lost its glow.
At the base of Pumori,
The oft told story,
Is just how much higher you can go.

Though you bask in the harmony of Tao,
Your confidence vanished somehow.
Probity announced its departure
How did it break and fall apart, sir?
Where's the road back to here and now?
It's time to abandon your futile quest,
The voices you're hearing know you best.
It's not just the loss of peace,
Or that you've been morally fleeced,
It's the taste of defeat you detest.

You've fought the fight,
You've won the race,
Now come and take your rightful place
In my kind, forgiving arms.
No talk of right or wrong
You're home now,
Right where you belong

*(**Zao:** Chinese for morning; good morning, suggesting a new day; a fresh start—**Tao:** The way, the path, the road to enlightenment.)*

28
TOTAL ECLIPSE

In the distance, just above the horizon,
Floating effortlessly through the morning mist,
Came the elegant apparition.
I turned my eyes easterly, unable to resist.

She wore a corsage of white
Around her frail and narrow wrist,
A symbol of her angelic purity
And the virtue I tried, in vain, to dismiss.

It may have been her unearthly glow,
Though it may have been the rising sun,
That shattered my fleeting reverie,
As the mournful day had scarcely begun.

I held on faintly to the feeling she evoked,
A fleeting moment I nearly missed;
A millisecond; a blink; a single synapse
Was just enough to savor her eternal bliss.

Then as quickly as she first appeared
She hastily turned and went,
Leaving me in the morning shadows
Spiritually drained, and emotionally spent.

We spent a day together, or two, it seemed,
And lost track of the lights we tripped.

She effortlessly opened up untold wounds
Buried deep within my stone-cold graveyard crypt.

My soul lay there, empty and bare,
Crying as I reminisced.
Counting the many chances I refused to take,
All the redheads I should have kissed.

We wandered through a labyrinth
Of the hedgerows' turns and twists,
Such an innocent encounter,
A tender and harmless tryst.

Along the way were scattered visions
Of all the things I'd missed:
Teaching me how to trust my heart
Instead of fighting with my fist;

To listen to the wiser voices of my soul;
To see with the hope of brightened eyes;
To face, with a firmness, all weaknesses and doubt;
To face the truth without compromise.

Then came a rare and haunting astral moment,
A phenomenon not to be missed.
Light and darkness tangled in a duel,
The mysterious solar eclipse.

Slowly, quietly the light began to dim
As if commanded to cease and desist.
It seemed the darkness overtook us
And illumination was, summarily, dismissed.

I may have been the only one on earth
Who didn't understand, or seem to care.
So iridescently unearthly
I looked heavenward on a dare.

"Look away, look away," she cried
As I stood defiantly unaware
Of the power of the larger light
And the blindness if you stare.

Then the blackness made a hasty retreat
"Away, be gone," the elements insist.
In the presence of the immortal light,
Darkness cannot peacefully coexist.

Believing I could not be mended,
Too badly broken to be fixed,
I was, for an instant, shown a fleeting glimpse
Of eternal light and never ending bliss.

29
ALONG THE EDGES

Spread your wings, oh spread your tender wings,
Let them lift you high above the fray.
Leave the small town behind you,
Turn and walk away,
So you can live to fight another day.

You got some bad news today
That came slowly along the wire.
It came without a precedent,
The circumstantial evidence,
Was ready to expire.

So there it was in black and white,
An invitation to the ball.
The bookie is taking all your bets,
Time to pass on your regrets,
Or answer the clarion call.

Spread your wings, oh spread your tender wings,
Let them lift you high above the fray.
Leave the small town behind you,
Turn and walk away,
So you can live and fight another day.

Take a side along the edges,
While you're young and innocent.
Tell them what they need to hear,

It doesn't have to be sincere
As long as it's expedient.

Recall that fateful, cloudy night,
That dubious incident,
All those intellectual binges,
That drove you to the fringes,
And the madness of your steep descent.

Spread your wings, oh spread your tender wings,
Let them lift you high above the fray.
Leave the small town behind you,
Turn and walk away,
So you can live and fight another day.

Keep telling your story again and again,
While you're still young and innocent.
Say it loud and say it clear,
It's the truth they want to hear
As they make believe it's all heaven sent.

Never mind about the details,
We've always known just what you meant.
Your tall tales were grand
When you marched and took a stand,
As self-righteousness came and then went.

Spread your wings, oh spread your tender wings,
Let them lift you high above the fray.
Leave the small town behind you,
Turn and walk away,
So you can live and fight another day.

Pack your grip and sail away--
Come to the party and dance.
Tell your mama that you must leave her;
But make sure you're a true believer;
Not just a victim of circumstance.

Spread your wings, oh spread your tender wings,
Let them lift you high above the fray.
Leave the small town behind you,
Turn and walk away,
So you can live and fight another day.

30
A THIRSTY BEDOUIN

I was born, the ancients say, with original sin,
A heavy burden for one as innocent as this.
I believed and carried that burden far too long--
I won't make that mistake again.

Looking back on all the places I have been,
The markers of a raggedy, random life,
And sudden u-turns uncounted.
Just one more, this time to make amends.

It's a long journey but I'm ready to begin
And walk in different furrows,
A wooden stick to aid my worried knees.
Tomorrow I'll start a brand-new regimen.

I walked out the door, prepared to take it on the chin
Under the roof of Andromeda
And the soulful contemplation
Of a modern, wandering, thirsty Bedouin.

I long ago lost touch with my patrilineal kin--
Arrogance, anger, resentment, jealousy--
I haven't a clue where it all went so wrong,
Or when the invisible permafrost set in.

I've was served a thousand writs of replevin
By friends who say I've done them wrong.
And while the accusations, at first, seemed credible,
The circumstantial evidence was mostly paper-thin.

Taken prisoner by a girl with the come-hither grin,
Though tortured, I didn't reveal a single thing,
Yet she always knew my innermost secrets
As if she was, somehow, my conjoined twin.

She was one part debutante, two parts harlequin,
And could speak with the blaring sound of a trumpet
Or with thunderous tympani rolls,
Yet, at times, with the calming voice of a well-tuned violin.

I want to find my story, the truth without spin.
Don't color it, don't embellish it,
Dish it up fresh and hot, nothing added,
Filled with one full-measure of chagrin.

I'm not an intellectual with a decorated sheepskin
But I can teach you the painful lessons of one man,
With neither head nor heart alone,
From a painful, years-long search from deep within.

I've walked the lonely road where boys turn into men
And wisdom isn't given but painfully earned.
So, here's hoping my weakened voice
Will somehow rise above the din.

The musty scrolls have followed me everywhere I've been,
The ancients smother me with the heavy weight of ages,
All the fabled myths on all those ancient pages
Have prompted in me, a much more modern sin.

"A poem is never finished, only abandoned."

PAUL VALERY

31
BREAK WITH PROTOCOL

The fork in the road beckons–
In time it comes to us all,
A fragile and weary voice,
A reckoning, a final choice,
And a courageous break with protocol.

"Join the revolution," they cried.
"Take an oath, stand tall, prepare to fight.
The final battle has begun,
We've got collegiality on the run,
The hostile victory is now within sight.

"It's expected that you'll stand with us,
We expect you to answer the call.
Forget your common sense,
Forget your independence,
From now on it's one for all."

There isn't a place here for indifference,
This is your wake-up call.
Ignore the naive audience,
Forget your inexperience,
And join the absurd free-for-all.

With a glaring youthful innocence
You got snared in their ragged trawl.
Stiff, as with rigor mortis,

Hoping, in vain, to make sense of this,
You tried to run before you could crawl.

You signed the binding contract,
Enraptured and enthralled.
Here's a word for the wise:
There's no room for compromise,
You're constrained for the very long haul.

So they tied you to a lamppost,
Firmly, with chain and ball.
The weight made you believe
That you could never leave.
Looks like you're a sycophant after all.

There are still so many mysteries
Locked in a musty room down the hall.
Wondering how it all made sense,
Not a single thought about recompense,
Only arrogant folly and chaotic falderal.

You've struggled with the role of a shill,
Like a mass-produced kewpie doll.
You may be lying, but don't knock it,
You're still carried around in their pocket,
Like a young, dependent marsupial.

So on you go, noble soldier,
You're ready to face the squall.
Revise the familiar old tactics,
There's a brand new approach to ethics:
A virus expanding its virulent sprawl.

There was very little real consolation,
Only the new and improved cattle call.
The cry seemed vaguely familiar,
Not what you wanted to hear
From the distant, obscene caterwaul.

Be confident and disregard facts,
The platform is completely overhauled.
Your credibility may be dying,
But, by any means, keep on denying.
Now it's obfuscate, deflect, and forestall.

The aged and rusty old ethos,
Seems hollow and empty overall.
But keep both faces smirking,
When honesty isn't working,
And beware; you may be asked to take the fall.

Your sincerity is so beguiling,
But it's a toxic new world after all.
The violent parry and thrust,
Left no one for you to trust,
And your grandiose visions hit the wall.

But maintain your cloud of evasiveness,
Cast a vaporous fog overall.
It may sound like hypocrisy,
But it's the brand new democracy,
And a new set of choices after all.

Now they're pressing forward confidently,
With a bold and unreserved gall.

But you saw, up ahead in the light,
The crumbling monument on the right,
Draped in a blackened funeral pall.

With a furious and unfettered arrogance,
They made ready the quadrennial brawl.
Knives unsheathed and drawn,
All the Kings and their plastic pawns,
Seemed poised for a drastic fall.

The long-sought victory is now DOA,
And integrity has gone AWOL.
Values are stored in the attic,
Ready for the next frontal attack,
Half bravura, and half Adderall.

There must have been some random mistake,
And your tuxedo has been mothballed.
Either simple oversight,
Or intentional sleight,
There's no room left at the governor's ball.

They may call you a coward, a fake, an imposter,
But set your feet, chin up, and stand tall.
Turn to the un-penitent crowd,
Tell the truth, shout it loud,
Kill the spotlight and break the fourth wall.

And then tell us all about the collapse,
Recount every gory detail you recall.
Retell us the colorful story,
The loss of an ancient glory,
And pride that comes before a fall.

32
BURN A BRIDGE

The meek, we are taught, will inherit the earth,
But it sounds patently absurd.
Those who inherit the earth,
Have an inestimable self-worth.
They're the strong and the bold, I've observed.

The poor in spirit have only one thing,
And that is, well, they're poor.
They're laggards, not leaders,
They're blue-vested Wal-Mart greeters.
The fearless and brave look for much more.

True leaders, the intrepid, and the fearless,
Are up front, ahead of the pack.
Never meek, quiet or bland,
They jump up, raise their voice, make a stand,
And smugly refuse to mind the gap.

They are the movers and shakers, the bold,
The confident, the gallant, the brave,
The difference makers,
The dangerous risk takers
Who violate norms and wantonly misbehave.

Take a chance, burn a bridge, make a clamor.
Charge fearlessly into the unknown.
Sharpen the sword,

Cut the cord,
Dive off cliffs, take a chance, claim the throne.

Old habits must sometimes die,
As the old rivers start to run dry.
Slit a few throats,
Burn a few boats,
Adjourn to the hills sine die.

Challenge every habit and norm.
Chuck the book, change the rules, set the pace.
No time for timidity,
Throw out the rigidity,
And never settle for second place.

Take no prisoners, lock behind you every gate
This is not the right time for diplomacy.
Like no conqueror before us,
You rewrote the hallelujah chorus,
Singing veni, vidi, vici.

The rules of the game are simple:
Disobey, disrupt, and destroy.
Set your feet, set the course,
Make ready the Trojan horse
As if you're marching on Troy.

 Never admit you're afraid.
Never let them see you sweat.
The passionate, brave, and courageous–
Those who've been branded audacious–
Press forward with little regret.

Shake off the jitters, nerves and fears,
If you're worried, don't ever show it.
A strong leader knows,
You occasionally step on some toes,
So step firmly, make sure they know it.

Make ready the colors and the breeches,
At daybreak, when the trumpet sounds.
Rally the pack,
Let the whip crack,
Mount up and release all the hounds.

The enemy is now on the run
Through the briars, the bushes, and brambles.
Without a paddle, the meek,
Are helplessly up the creek,
Their dispirited brigade in shambles.

When the battle is finally won,
And you're the only one that remains.
Consider the worth of the cause,
Without caution or pause,
Take the hill, plant a flag, stake your claim.

Take your rightful place at the helm,
Saddle up, grab the reigns, take the lead.
You quickened the pace,
Now take your rightful place,
The chase is over, el mapache has been treed.

"A POEM begins as a lump in the throat, a sense of wrong, a homesickness, a lovesickness."

ROBERT FROST

33
THE PREACHER IN THE VILLAGE SQUARE

The man in the village preached, but I couldn't hear.
His hand painted sign said the end is near.
What an odd thing, I thought, teaching with fear,
But the small crowd seemed robotic and bored.

His once-white robes were weathered and gray.
I see him, without fail, preaching every day.
He's completely at ease doing things his way
With little thought of an eternal reward.

His rantings, wild, rambling, unorthodox,
Standing there on his makeshift preacher's box,
Keeping track of the end-of-the-earth world clocks,
Re-setting them on a whim to suit his needs.

The warnings I saw changed a little here and there.
He didn't bother with facts, didn't know, didn't care.
He suspected the world was hopelessly lost and unaware,
So, he lived by his custom-made creed.

He had a convert in me that day
As I began thinking about what he was trying to say.
We both saw things in a similar way,
Though his motives were, perhaps, a bit more pure.

I told him of the pain I had endured,
And though he never uttered a single word
He made my questions sound simple and absurd,
Leaving me shaky, unstable, and a little unsure.

He offered me a piece of sound advice,
That I needed no golden calf to sacrifice,
And with a single roll of his loaded dice
I felt ready to settle all bets.

Suddenly I heard a choir begin to sing,
Fearing this may be my final day of reckoning.
My attempt at blind faith couldn't remove the bitter sting
Or erase the burden of my heavy debt.

Gone, for an instant, my hurtful enmity,
Gone all the guilt-induced, non-verbal profanity,
Still clinging to the worldview of vanity
As I rethought all the ancient laws.

The choir sang their soothing melodies,
In four/four time of earthly calamities,
His dire warnings multiplied with such ease,
Who knows what the ancients really saw?

We are told to blindly stand and genuflect,
With motives that, to some, seem circumspect,
Completely devoid of any self-respect
And the countenance of a Pagliacci clown.

Accused and made the primary suspect
In the war with a dubious underground sect,
I began hoping for a little bit more respect

From the ones I disappointed and let down.

Turn off the microphone, camera and lights,
It's not a battle of who's wrong or who's right.
Were all still guided by the very same light,
And comfortable with the choices we've made.

The choir's benediction came much too soon,
The children had already left the room.
A list of large numbers from the baby boom
Remained uncounted and mostly unafraid.

Now I'm standing on a box custom made just for me,
My sign in large red letters for all the world to see,
Taking my turn, standing firm, standing valiantly.
Turns out I have what I needed all along.

The old man in the village knew where he belonged,
He was faithful, vigilant, and strong,
And I knew we had little chance to get it right
If we constantly tell others they're completely wrong.

"What is a **POET**? An unhappy person who conceals profound anguish in his heart, but whose lips are so formed that, as sighs and cries pass over them, they sound like beautiful **music**."

SOREN KIERKEGAARD

34
AQUA MOLTO BELLA

One of these days,
One of these wet, drizzle days,
To make sure you're still alive,
Step outside and feel the rain,
Breath deeply, take it in, revive.
Take your pulse, leave your pride,
Leave the umbrella,
Come outside,
And step into the pouring rain.
Have no fear,
I'm standing right here.
I understand and feel your pain.

Break free of your cage,
Leave your cubical prison behind.
Stomp in a puddle, take a dive
Into the madness of the unrehearsed.
Why not? You'll survive.
Join the chaos of the unabashed
How can things get much worse?
What happened to playing it safe?
It's waiting in the big, black hearse.
Look up to the clock in the tower
And keep on dancing,
It's running in reverse.

It may look like an unfamiliar rain,
A storm you've never seen before.
It's a cloudburst of the unexpected,
It's the deluge of the uninhibited.
The fragrance of try once more.
Time to let go of doubt and timidity,
Your fear of getting wet,
Of exposing your borderline insanity
In the rainstorm of no regrets.
Come outside, open your eyes and see
The strength of this summer shower,
And the cleansing power of its purity.

It's not just another summer shower,
It's a torrent of clarity,
It's a flood of inspiration,
And cleansing of your vanity.
It's a cloudburst for the skeptic,
Renewal for the weary of heart,
New life for the timid, the trembling,
The river of a brand new start.
The rain will leave you clean,
Baptized and fully immersed
In the fountain of remorse,
And the conformity you've always cursed.

Dancing in the rain!
Look, You did it;
You're bravely dancing in the pouring rain--

Gene Kelly never looked this good–
Nothing ventured, everything to gain.
It's the dance of starting over,
I always knew you could.
Your dance is a rain-washed Pas de Duex;
An innocent misbehavior,
But see what you're able to do
From this refreshing new vista,
And an elevated point of view.

Keep dancing in the water
Though you're soaking wet
From your head down to your feet.
The improv got you moving,
The rhythm calming and soothing,
Confidently, carelessly incomplete.
Unencumbered and free,
You found your balance
And mastered the arabesque.
Come let the water flow,
Wash away the frightening tableau
That once seemed so Kafkaesque.

Discard the DeLorme mask you wear,
Fearlessly take the rainy stage.
Confidently bask in the shimmering glare,
Celebrate the miracles that come
With the cleansing of fear and despair.
Comes the rain with its healing power,
Such an unexpected surprise,
The alchemy of an urban shower.

Come live with me in the moment,
Such a balm for urban anxiety.
There's a promise of atonement
In the flash flood of spontaneity.

Let the rain wash over you,
Let conformity run its course,
Others will listen and respect what you do
As they find their own founts
And take a chance on what's different and new.
As you stand there, soaking wet,
Make a hard right turn,
An unexpected pirouette.
Let the rain wash your face, drench your hair,
Lift burdens off your shoulder.
Act child-like without worry or care,
But hurry, you're already one day older.

Come and stand with me in the pouring rain,
Join the thunder and lighting revolution.
A storm as redeeming as this
Carries a promise of absolution.
Ignore all that's expected,
Tear up the handbook and all the rules,
You may soon be reborn or resurrected,
And you've outwitted all the fools.
Throw down your umbrella,
Forget your rubber boots,
Come dance the barefoot dance
Of aqua molto bella.

"A Poem
begins as a lump
in the throat,
a sense of wrong,
homesickness,
a lovesickness."

ROBERT FROST

35
ASTROPHOBE

I climb away from the city lights,
A step or two higher each night,
Until the noise of the visual litter is gone.
My lofty new vantage point
Becomes just a vanishing point,
Washed away in the deluge of the amber dawn.

The mariners speak in reverent code:
"Don't miss the moon in full-corn mode.
The wolf-moon with its ancient call."
I'm a fully converted equinoxian,
Connecting with humans once again,
Close to losing a grip, and risking a tragic fall.

Caught between the Northern Lights
And the warm Southern nights,
And the range of illumination in between,
There was some unintentional sleight,
And I was read my legal rights,
But released when they found my record clean.

But I'm still an avid gazer every night,
Can't be arrested for seeking the light,
Or searching for edges of this earthly globe.
Solemn in the overwhelming vastness of the night,
With never a beginning or an end in sight,
Confessing fears in the cathedral of the astrophobe.

Cautious in the pale starlight,
Terrified by astral witnesses of the night,
How could I possibly know?
The blackness of the endless black.
Washes over me and takes me back
To that forgotten, primordial glow.

I've never found the outer limit,
Nor any other life-form within it,
No edge, no wall, no end in sight.
As I ponder the vast immensity,
The blackness becomes just another fence to me,
And distance, gratefully, is measured in light.

Earthly specks gaze upward, demanding
Knowledge and answers, yet never understanding
The power of the light and its intensity.
The end of my search is at last in sight,
I will find you if you'll send up a light.
Without you, nothing feels like home to me.

The chill of the winter solstice
Pulled us apart and somehow tossed us.
I don't know how far away you really are.
You're not lost, just out of sight,
But I'm coming, I'll follow the light
Of your forgiving, personal lodestar.

The brightness of the star-flung skies
Will always shine clearly in the depths of your eyes,
And, yet, you're still so many light years away.
I'm certain your love was, to me, heaven sent,
I'll find you, all navigation extant,
As the power of the universe begs me stay.

36
CONTRADICTION BLUES

I'm a walking contradiction
In everything I say and do.
I've tried to choose one side or the other
But it's hard to be consistent
When ideas come from deep inside of you,
For the most part, an opposing point of view.

This is how I am, quite naturally,
Obtuse, wavering, and contrary.
I'll very likely find a thing or two,
And strongly disagree
When I take my final rest
And edit my own obituary.

I live right here on contradiction avenue,
Every house the same shade of beige,
Except mine, an unearthly pinkish hue.
I haven't any flowers and never trim my trees,
Never pull a weed, I don't see the need.
Why plant a green lawn when a load of gravel will do.

I've got a life-long case of contradiction blues,
I've walked far too long in a pair of contradiction shoes.
One wants to take me way up North,
The other wants to head down South,
And my friends say you've got contradictions
Coming out both sides of your mouth.

I've got a bad case of contradiction disease,
And a wobbly pair of contradiction knees.
I take them to church on Sunday and pray,
But when I rise and face a brand-new day,
I revert to my more natural contradictory ways
And do whatever the hell I please.

I'm just a walking contradiction
Singing the wildly popular contradiction blues.
There is no cure for this complicated malady.
No hope as far as I can see.
I win virtually any argument
Regardless of which side I choose

I own two contradictory television sets
One gets a signal from the east,
The other from the west.
I turn them on looking for a little good news
But get only opinion and biased views--
Worthless dreck, nothing I can use.

I've reserved a seat in the contradictory pews,
Hearing strange ideas from this contradictory milieu,
Reviewing ancient mores
And a contradictory pile of stories
That now seem badly out of touch,
Inconsistent with the more traditional Good News.

So, the reverend stopped by to see me,
Called me to a sore repentance
And told me there was still time
To lose the devil and choose the divine,

But I caught him recently behind the church
Drinking all the sacramental wine.

I live in a contradictory country,
Some red states, some blues.
Take a side, pick either side,
Doesn't matter which one you choose,
This is a new breed of politicians
And either way, you're guaranteed to lose.

I have a set of contradictory eyes.
You may see in them the honest truth,
Or they may hide little white lies.
Sometimes they dance, sometimes they cry
But don't gaze too deeply
And pierce my thin disguise.

I have a pair of contradictory arms
One left, of course, the other on the right.
One is ready for a warm embrace,
The other poised for a dangerous fight.
One to push you gently away,
One to hold you through the most dismal night.

I have a contradictory heart
One with the hope of a new love,
The other crushed before it can start.
One that is bitter, icy cold,
One that can have the softer, kinder part,
One that is confident, brave and bold.

When they took me to the courthouse,

The judge handed down his final decree:

"It's against the law to carry a protest sign,

We expect you to simply toe-the-line.

Son, you're a frightening menace to society.

We find you guilty: Contradiction in the first degree."

37
TRUTH OR DARE

I don't have all the answers,
But you don't really seem to care.
Perhaps you're over confident
Because it's your private game of truth or dare.

You say you're looking for honest men,
Who shout warnings to "beware."
You've found the voices who will take your side,
And follow you anywhere.

You rejected all the news reports,
Took a righteous and daring stand,
Endured the noise of the kangaroo court,
And the very public reprimand.

You found me in a curious state,
Warned by others to prepare
For your devious and clever ways,
And the badge of courage you always wear.

I've tried hard to avoid you,
And the traps you set around your lair.
You gave so little thought to recklessness,
Or whom you might ensnare.

Storm the catwalk with your practiced flourish,
Make them turn their heads and stare.
Fill them with admiration,
But don't leave the cupboards bare.

You have your version of integrity,
And the virtue you always wear,
Your periscope is finding new realities
Underwater and blindly unaware.

Step into the batter's box,
Take a curve ball if you dare.
Instant replay will never reveal
If the ball you hit is foul or fair.

With all the sycophants in tow,
Everyone you meet will know
The true and faithful lemmings--
The voices of your definitive manifesto.

I couldn't give you all the answers,
On our train to who knows where,
I couldn't finish the Q. and A.
And I didn't have the right fare.

I'm finished standing behind you,
In your shadow or in the glare.
Fearlessness becomes you
Behind the façade you always wear.

Ignore everything you've ever learned,
Machiavellian ways have returned.
Along the shores of the Rubicon,
The warrior boats have all been burned.

You beat me to the punch most times,
I have so little time to prepare.
You're so quick with the buzzer,
And the rules are extraordinaire.

You've seen the writing on the scrolls,
They've turned up everywhere,
But you can't see the writing on the walls,
Not a helpful clue anywhere.

Make a speech, ignite the crowd,
Say it clear and say it loud.
Only one voice is allowed,
Don't blow it, make us proud.
Say it simply, say it honestly,
Then humbly take your bow.
No more encores,
Just one final curtain call,
At least for now.

38
LOOKING FOR THE SCRAPBOOK

The battered old farmhouse,
Linoleum floor badly worn,
The harvest was in,
The sheep were shorn,
And the berries were off the vine.

Pink mums were all that remained,
The soil amended, churned, tilled,
The country garden loved, pruned,
A muted palette for the autumn chill
In this unforgiving clime.

The little white house, cobbled together,
Crooked, cracked, forlorn,
An extra room added in front,
Patched, painted, reborn,
A Polaroid of the simpler time.

A dark brown stove huddles in the living room,
Logs and coal its steady winter diet.
Thanksgiving, nights craving more lumps
To warm my feet as I lay beside it
The whole night through.

No bed, just a bag on the floor,
No pillow, just an elbow,
I know this is where I belong

At the feet that walked here ages ago,
So many things I wished I knew.

The blissful days, the simple ways,
Worn out denim knees,
A thirty-foot tire-swing
Hung between to towering Poplar trees
Carried us far, far away.

Horse-drawn tractors, wooden yokes,
Abandoned in the apple orchard, in the rear.
Lower the rusted plows, bring ancient dirt alive,
A 1900's vintage John Deere
Come back to life for a single day.

Threadbare shirts and Converse shoes,
Patches on faded denim.
Herding cows and sailing boats
Sunup to sundown, satisfying every curious whim
But one. Or two.

The adult conversations, cryptic calls,
Hushed voices, whispers, never minds.
Stop asking questions, it's not your concern.
There are things best left behind,
Out of reach, out of view.

Nothing villainous, scandalous, criminal,
Family knots, twisted, kept from innocent eyes.
Tragic longings, heartaches, fears, tears,
Not quite the truth, not quite lies,
Dust behind the hardwood pew.

For answers that we needed
We pried, snooped and spied
In the attic, cupboards, shelves, garages,
To find where the secrets hide.
Lost? Tossed? Burned?

No hints, signs, maps, no answers,
Diligently, innocently trying to find a single clue
To answer our questions.
The whys and hows and who
Had come and gone; spurned.

On the roof a feeble TV antenna,
Ravaged by the storm,
No picture, no afternoon soaps.
Twisted, turned, windblown,
Selective viewing, restive weather.

Nothing but aluminum static.
Grandpa says climb up, turn it west.
The smell of mothballs in the musty attic.
In the corner, cobwebs, dust, asbestos,
A large red book bound in leather.

The photos, the stories, the missing pages,
The long-awaited look into the past,
The snooping, the digging, the none of your business
Recovered, uncovered at last.
Take a breath, take a look.

Take a seat, wipe the dust, sneeze.
Our questions were of the desperate kind.
The oversized, heavy book on denim knees,
The answers we longed to find.
But it's a hollow, empty book.

Brittle plastic pages crack, crumble
Beneath naive fingers,
Inquisitive, brave, still humble,
Lacking wise eyes to see,
A cheap antenna, ears poorly attuned.

The key we thought would unlock cages—
This hidden trove we hadn't seen before--
Not a single truth left on the yellowed pages,
Removed, taken, not there anymore.
How far, how long, by whom?

Family history genetically modified,
Scarcely a hint along the edges,
Truths and lies, side by side,
Mercurochrome and bandages
Won't heal gaping wounds nor seal the bloody gashes.

The book is still here, empty, aged.
Where have all the flowers gone?
What havoc tore apart the pages?
Truth is not where it belongs.
Open the brown furnace, sift the ashes.

The tumult and the arrogance of memories,
Carefully trimmed, taped, preserved, glued,
Once held together DNA strands,
Ancestral blood running through you.
Stories erased, evidence never shown.

Lovingly repair the old farmhouse,
Too few shingles, far too many leaks.
Replace the broken bedroom window,
Nail floorboards where they creak.
If only walls could speak, and groan.

39
BAREFOOT ON CONCRETE

The show had a title, and a story in place,
(A famous author was giving it birth).
The lead actor had the right name, pedigree, and face,
For this tale of bad taste, and dubious worth.

They wrote it with me as chief antagonist,
Then, re-wrote, and polished the troubled script.
I wasn't first or fourth, not even tenth choice on their list.
Scrub the numbers, hush-hush, tight-lipped.

I detested the lead actor and, at first, refused,
Two arch-rivals from the very start.
Other than a deep, long-standing hatred, I had no excuse,
And reluctantly agreed to play the part.

He was a man so easy to dislike, disdain, easy to hate,
And despise even more over time.
Brought together by a cruel and unforgiving fate,
Perhaps by the devil's own design.

All about him, all around him,
Every tic, every blink, every gesture annoyed,
While clouds of darkness would surround him
In an inky cloak of schadenfreude.

Every word, every fake tear, every pregnant pause,
Rehearsed and uniformly despised,
I knew, first hand, his moods and all his faux pas,
But leave it to the audience decide.

His footprints like a sidewinder track in the sand,
The dank smell of venom all around,
All pretense at collegiality be damned,
He slithered onto the stage, a serpent, without a sound,

Crawled under a rock, his best disguise,
A dark, foreboding place to lay,
Where his forked tongue and menacing eyes
Patiently awaited his terrified, unsuspecting prey.

His appearance seemed haggard, hammered, and weathered,
His pallor bordering on a pale, whitish-green,
His demeanor un-tucked, unraveled, and untethered,
And, with yellow eyes, massacred every scene.

His voice was grating and sandpaper rough,
Like summer bare feet walking on concrete.
Incessant carping was boundless--though never enough--
From his stage-right balcony seat.

His tirades were filled with ill-timed bombast,
This would be a long, slow, one-sided decay.
When everyone on the stage had finally been trashed,
Emotions were dispatched and sent on their way.

Across the stage, now, from his chief antagonist,
Floating in as if a thistle seed on a breeze,
He fired the first volley or two, but badly missed,
And fell victim to vitriol and sleaze.

He spoke with an acerbic and confident cadence,
His words were calculated, measured, and terse,
As the spirits stood by him in the afternoon séance,
He knew every line, delivered as if an ancient voodoo curse.

He was less concerned with the details of reality,
Focused on his grand entrance and his appearance.
Under the spotlight of genetically-engineered vanity,
He pierced egos with mace, sword, and lance.

He could put on a dazzling, award-winning performance,
Add fire to any dark, lonely soliloquy,
Though it became just a self-hypnotized trance
That no one wanted to hear, no one wanted to see.

He seemed badly out of character, this viper in his hole,
Hiding behind wigs, makeup, and costumes.
The only thing missing was passion, heart, and soul--
Waiting for inert emotions to be exhumed.

But something about this overwrought script,
Lacked even a shred of warmth and humanity,
Like a horse that's been badly whipped,
He obediently paraded his aging and forlorn banality.

The method-actor with the porcelain soul,
Made the patrons writhe in their seats.
He'd waited his entire life for this juicy role,
His downward spiral now nearly complete.

It was straight-jacket invective he sprayed on the crowd,
An unrestrained diatribe, vile and perverse.
The entire audience, it appeared, all prayed out loud.
His deep, inner-loathing well timed, well rehearsed.

The stage, instantly, became a red-striped revival tent
As he entered with his massive ego in tow.
Shredded the script, then off he went
Into the fire-breathing carnival freak show.

All his lines now a whisper, his last dramatic breath,

No one could understand, or feel his pyrrhic art.

So he died the painful, forgotten-actors' death,

And the show ended before it could start.

The show must go on, and will go on, ad infinitum.

There's a new chapter in this well used book.

The right script will thrill and excite them,

Because everything deserves a second look.

Everyone's an actor, anyone can rise or fall,

And play for pathos, tragedy, or a laugh.

But it's jealousy, envy, rage, and vitriol

That soiled the red carpet and slaughtered the golden calf.

40
DALI'S DILEMMA

You've struggled with the push I gave you.
A gentle bump, a nudge.
You resented my suggestions,
When I played both jury and judge.

I may have tried to change you too much,
You were so melancholy and content.
Perhaps I saw a bit more in you,
And you misunderstood my intent.

> *There's a faith you'll need to muster,*
> *A hope you'll need to summon.*
> *It's in conformity and complacency*
> *That you've become unwittingly common.*

You reprised and memorized your early roles,
But that production has come and gone.
Time to write a brand-new chapter,
Time for you to briskly move along.

You've been fleeced, your pockets emptied,
The victim of an elaborate con
While you were sorting out the roles
Deciding who plays the king and pawn?

> *It doesn't have to be a choice*
> *Between your God and mammon;*
> *It's you alone that decides if your voice*
> *Will be ordinary or uncommon.*

You struggled to decide between
Fitting in or standing out,
And never took a sharp u-turn
To see what courage is all about.

You always chose to dress in fashion,
Your hair, your makeup and jeans,
Preferring to be near the safety net
Of conformity, it seems.

> *Take a page from the book of Rand,*
> *Or the wisdom of King Solomon.*
> *It's in conformity and complacency*
> *That we all become so common.*

You always followed every one-way sign,
And obeyed all the rules you could,
Never taking the road less travelled
That diverges in the yellow wood.

You mapped it out and stayed the course,
Never craving fortune or fame.
Individuality vanished somewhere,
And conformity took the blame.

> *Take a page from the book of Rand,*
> *Or the wisdom of King Solomon;*
> *It's in conformity and complacency*
> *That we all become so common.*

For you there were no Dylans, Dalis or Degas,
Afraid to break the rules and laws.
But you never walked the razor's edge
Believing conformity is such a noble cause.

Afraid to get up on the stage,
Afraid of the brightness of the lights,
Afraid to take the box in Hyde Park,
Afraid to run, afraid to stay and fight.

   It doesn't take a long-haired genius,
   Or the wisdom of King Solomon,
   But it does require you to chose
   To be extraordinary or end up common.

No sense in being brave anymore,
Your future's been foretold,
It's somewhere in your little, red, rule book,
Do exactly what you've been told.

Let's take you home tonight
And tuck you safely into your cozy bed.
You may have already forgotten
Any of the dreams that once swirled in your head.

   Take a page from the book of Rand,
   Or the wisdom of King Solomon--
   It's in conformity and complacency
   That we all become so ordinary, so common.

41
FOLLOWING CAIRNS

The road before me has far too many twists and turns,
And craggy, black lava boulders mark the way.
The air is gauzy thin, each breath a painful burn—
Not exactly what I had in mind today.
The old man of red-mountain seems bitter-cold, taciturn.
It's cowardly to turn around, too ominous to stay.

Following directions of every well-placed cairn,
Carefully pushing boulders straight up hill,
Missing, by just inches, the vital first and ten,
If you don't complete the trek right now, you likely never will.
Listen to the messages the pathway markers send,
Or remain a silent coward, inert and deathly still.

Relying on the ancient, mystic power of Zen
To show you footsteps, there, along the shore,
And taking stock it's meaning every now and then,
Strengthened, not weakened by the load you daily bore.
Difficult to know how, impossible to know when,
Feeling as if you've somehow walked this trail before.

Ancient footsteps below, whisper a plaintive call,
Ignored, forgotten, and daily desecrated,
Where flash-flood torrents carved the canyon walls,
Left the riparian floor wounded, decimated,
With jagged edges that portend a tragic fall,
Yet in time, renewed, revived, and re-created.

Step cautiously, and leave your alms,
Follow carefully the cairn-marked trail.
Touch, feel, embrace the ancient healing balm,
Wash clean your burdens and trials,
Breathe in the peaceful, forgiving calm,
As you walk these unforgiving, torturous miles.

Feel it, live it, until, at last, you return.
Remember every rugged peak, every stream you had to ford,
Hear again the echoes of the secrets you have learned,
The wisdom of the canyons safely stored
In a red-clay, Anasazi urn.
Now you've banished the invading Mongol hordes
To a point of no return,
As they make a shameful retreat back to Karakorum
And every bridge has burned.

42
HER BIRTHSTONE WAS AMETHYST

Her birthstone was Amethyst,
The rare, violet gem,
Jewel of purple light,
The intriguing, the coveted, the dangerous diadem.
Brightest in the day,
Diminished by the night.
Unlike any other earthly color,
It elevated and set her apart, alone,
Authorized her heavenly calling,
Her foreordained birthright is all she's ever known.
Seemingly unaware of the simmering unrest,
She waltzed in to power and captured the ancient throne
Under the aegis of the royal Amethyst.

Born under the sign of the Aquarian,
She risked her mortal sanity,
Summoned the humility of one who is heaven blessed,
Tentatively, pondering the vastness of her kingdom
And the riches, the power she would now possess.
Born again she donned the purple robes,
Threw off the shackles of doubt
And became the woman she had never been,
With power she could only dream about.
She banished all her lovers,

Erased traces of every ill-advised tryst,
And sought the forgiving power, absolution
From the royal amethyst.

Possessed of neither a keen intellect,
Nor much of wisdom collected through the years,
No clever repartee, humor, or insight
That even shrewd intelligentsia could detect.
No passionate oratory, no tall tales to delight,
No sweeping, self-defense scheme,
No grand manifesto,
Very little of enduring self-esteem.
Little interest in the finer points of law,
She dispossessed her earthly flaws,
Thoroughly and innocently bewitched
By the mythical revelations
Of the royal amethyst.

Under purple skies and purple rain,
Under heaven's watchful care,
With little understanding of mortal suffering and pain,
Or the simmering contempt
Of the diminished crowd,
And a festering anger never uttered out loud,
There arose a deafening chant she believed was love,
Though, in truth, just an ancient, wretched disdain.
She would rule under a heavy cloud, a blotchy purple stain.
Inebriated by the adoration,
Drunken by the lingering myths,
The haunting, mysterious purple glow
Of the powerful amethyst.

With an itinerant preacher's zeal,
Devoid, completely, of a beating heart,
Oblivious to how the crowd may feel,
Deciding on caprice, on whims,
Who loses, who wins.
Raising prices for forgiveness,
Quick to dispatch the ample noose,
She became the sole, authorized arbiter,
No hope, no pardons, no appeals, no commutation.
She ruled from the bench--her high and holy station--
As if with an iron fist.
Every verdict validated
By the assumed power of the royal amethyst.

Awash in the constant glow of the cabochon,
Her dazzling, obscene display,
Brilliant in the light of day,
Overexposure dimmed its bright rays
And watched them slowly to turn to gray.
The more the jewel was exposed,
The more its brightness began to slip away.
Nature's laws could not be changed,
Earthly elements, she learned, will never obey
The empty bargaining,
And her incessant, prayerful requests.
Such was the feeble, fainting power
Of the arrogant amethyst.

She always wore one in her bracelet--
The dark Siberian amethyst--
And hung another around her narrow neck
And, from a tower, faced her loyal subjects,
Demanding their loyalty and feudal respect.
She dreamed it was admiration,
Prayed it was adoration.
But this regal, vaporous queen,
Whom the throngs openly detest,
Lost her way in the glare,
The gauzy unremitting light
And the confusing signals
Of the mysterious amethyst.

There were other things around her throat
The peasants wished to see:
A heavy rope, a noose,
The gleaming blade of the guillotine.
A slash from ear to ear
Rendering her history an obscure footnote.
There arose a bloodletting coup, a reprieve
For the peasants, a relief from suffocating fear,
To rid the kingdom of the tyrants
Who ruled not with law but of superstition
And the entitlement they pretend to detest.
She hides behind the God-given power,
The dubious anointing,
By the righteous amethyst.

She never fully understood the strength
Of the gray men standing behind the throne,
Of governing, of ruling, of decrees,
Of sovereignty and the chains of slavery.
So many things she daily dismissed,
Absorbed by the intoxicating power,
And temptations no mortal woman could resist,
She was drawn into the royal, deranged logic,
With all its turns and twists,
Drowning in a deluge of greed,
Dragged under by the tide,
Pulled down by the unrelenting force

Of the burdensome amethyst.
The bleak and rigid throne
Grew wearisome and discomfiting,
And the gray men plotted and conspired
To find a witless, passive consort--
A kingly puppet on a string.
And while the voices of the angry dissidents
Fell on her tone-deaf, virginal ears,
She remained aloof, an icy diffidence,
Keeping silent her growing mortal fears,
Quashing rumors, hiding frequent tears.
All marionettes summarily dismissed
And banished from the kingdom
By final decree from the powerful amethyst.

She retreats to the comfort of her isolation
And the search for the perfect face to wear.
Which personality to chose,
What unwitting prey to ensnare,
What temporary relationships to lose.
And the oracle of the purple stone,
Unpredictable and dichroic,
Artfully deflected and split the light,
Leaving her listless, defeated and stoic,
Restless and tragically unheroic.
Her two faces, now, could no longer coexist,
A painful reprimand, a scold,

A gentle rebuke of the maternal amethyst.
A thousand and one amethyst stones
Lined her protective shield.
A thousand, perhaps two thousand more
Sewn into her violet and lilac robes
And the lavish, lavender gowns she always wore.
The precious stone surrounded her hand-held mirror:
The window of her royal vanity.
The jewels glittered on walls, a dancing light,
Illuminating hidden passageways, tunnels into the night,
And daily escapes from queenly insanity.
Purple gems surround her empty bed,
And bedecked the heavy purple crown
She anxiously wore upon her head.

Always a gaudy show of riches,
Every stone conspicuously arrayed,
Reflecting stories of the ages
And the power she believed they conveyed.
At every state affair and earthly fest,
Came the arrogant and ill-advised display
Of the powerful amethyst.
Soon enough the deplorables would all understand
The saga of a simple girl ascended to the purple throne,
Alone and hobbled by unrelenting duress,
Addicted, now, to the power
Of the hypnotic amethyst.

She tried, in vain, to open the seventh seal,
Failing, flailing, and falling again and again,
Listening for salvation in the church bells' peal,
She calculated how to pillage the treasury
And anything else she could steal.
Then rounded up the muted dissidents
Crying in the corners of their musty knaves,
The paean of the faithful, the simple lament,
The cry of the hungry, the indentured slaves.
Hobbled by unexplained seizures and fits,
Concealing her plentiful, rapacious trysts,
A new era had begun:
The reign of the powerful amethyst.

She believed the gems would end her anxiety--
The healing power of the phony purple gem
Wash away the clinging sorrow; revive her piety,
Alleviate the unrelenting torment of distress
And her precise, calculated, royal regimen.
Lacking, longing for the renewal of love's warm caress,
She summoned up the revelations of what may lie ahead;
A tentative but prophetic look into the future
For the key to unlock, forever more,
The heavy burdens of her manacled wrists,
Finding solace, finding comfort
In the healing balm of the sacred stone,
The tender and forgiving amethyst.

It was that transcendent, radiant beauty
Caught deep inside the facets,
The hypnotic purple beams
That danced along the jewelry's royal crest,
And haunted all her dreams.
The dark violet and the lavender hues
Gave the royal emblems an air of authority,
The light of gods and kings,
Embedded in the royal crest
Became the protective armor
She wore about her breast.
The blessing of the heavens
Forever captured in the holy amethyst.

That jewel of rare, unearthly color,
She of cunning and little remorse,
Wore it like the tyrant queen she had become,
Addicted to it's magic, a thrice daily, lethal dose.
Regal in her jewel bedecked crown
She walked on obscure roads of authority,
Hers alone, from on high was handed down,
Leaving her hated, scorned by the vassal throngs,
Resented by the shrinking middle class,
Loved by all the rest
Who reverently bowed to the fractured light
And bathed in every shard,
The allure of the cunning amethyst.

The stone was daily set before her.
She was wrapped and adorned in her insular piety.
On bended knee she humbly sought
Truth, honesty, honor, and humility,
Trapped in the angles and sharp edges
And hidden in the fractals of the gems' reality.
The promise of endless glory, on her bestowed,
Entombed there in the warm, inviting purple glow,
For her, the naïve, restless woman, a secret code.
Acting out her well rehearsed pretense,
The translucent folly of the innocent
Seemed such a pointless quest.
Outwitted, again at the tempting shine,
Caught in the trap of the ruthless amethyst.

Sequestered behind purple walls
She cancelled all official duties and chores,
No pleadings, no telegrams, no red-phone calls,
Refusing the duties of state she so abhors.
Sitting alone and ponderously aloof,
Back ramrod straight, eyes forward, head erect,
She had no one to see, nowhere to go,
No armed conflicts to direct,
No gawking public sideshow.
Not a shred of guilt or sorrow
The conniving, gray men could detect.
Locked and stowed safely away
In the prison of the amethyst.

No need for treaties with allies;
No invitation, no Nobel peace award;
No need for the media's exaggerated stories;
No ancient feuds to suppress;
No conquering of the Mongol hordes;
No rival factions to oppress.
An occasional severed head lay on her table--
Something real and tangible she could detest.
Hated and scorned by the indentured class,
But loved by those who thought they knew her best,
The fawning ants devoted to their queen.
"Come," she cries. "Raise the sacred, purple goblet,
Intricately carved from ancient amethyst."

Now she cowers behind the impenetrable fence.

No newsreel, no speeches or spotlight,

Only somber penitence.

No jealous heart to steal.

No glaring, envying, greedy eyes,

No broken heart to conceal.

No halcyon days, no neon nights.

Safely stowed away from the internecine fights,

The truth was at last revealed--

As the jester and the wizard would attest--

The royal color always faded under too much light,

Gone the captivating glow

Of the dying amethyst.

Comes the dawn

Eerily washed in lavender's luring light.

There is blood, now, flowing in the street,

And purple-painted epithets scarring the palace walls.

The working class gathered in the marketplace

And huddled behind the fetid stalls.

Their tepid, simmering anger

Became a burgeoning and confident protest,

The long foretold flash point of a purple revolution

Against the tyranny of the iron fist,

A rejection of the crippled reign

And the imminent downfall

Of the fabled, and fraudulent amethyst.

There arose a new color, a new banner,
A new voice, resonant and clear.
The chant of the forgotten,
The promise of a new day without fear,
With the vision of a different dawn,
The purple light began at last to disappear,
So too the pathos of the tired, the weary, the pawn.
Hope alone now flooded the streets.
The royal court toppled, tyranny on the run,
The failed and vanquished queen,
Under the ignominy of house arrest,
Gone the glow, forever dimmed,
The specious machinations of the purple amethyst.

"Hand me the royal amulet", she pleads,
"And let me once more wear it to battle.
Drape me one last time in purple robes.
Let me inspire the troops, ignite their passion
That I may hear again the sabers rattle.
Let loyal subjects kiss again the bony finger,
That was once an iron fist,
Which so blindly clung to the all-knowing amethyst.
As the darkness of years begin to blind,
Let me not tarry in darkness alone.
Lay beside me on the lilac pillow, the sacred stone,
As I take my final rest,
That I may be forever remembered, loved, revered,
Eternally bathed in the dying embers
Of the once strong and mighty amethyst."

43
METALLIC DROSS

He had been going, for some time,
Through a difficult phase
That everyone believed would pass.
But it stayed and stayed,
And did little to improve his awkward ways,
And the nasty habits he amassed,
That elsewhere, in earlier days,
Would have been adjudged to be a crime.

He wandered about the empty spaces,
Broken windows, boarded passageways,
Empty eyes, hollow faces,
And found comfort there.
Though desolation was everywhere,
His mind began to selectively erase
Even brief glimpses of halcyon days,
Now vanished without a trace.

He couldn't remember his simple crusade,
And failed a simple recall test of his abuses
Of protocol, and all the normal rules
That he twisted and bent at will.
He believed he had taken the hill
That led to the cave of fools,
Tangled in his painfully weak excuses
And his troubling, real-world escapades.

He believed in wandering off the path,
Deliberately going against the grain.
Then, suddenly, found himself too far afield,
Looking desperately for the next cairn.
No clue about where and when
His ego had, scandalously, been killed,
Leaving nothing but skeletal remains,
Lost, forever, in the noisy aftermath.

There was still the border to cross,
And empty silos yet to fill.
Failing to meet the standard quota,
He came back despised and empty handed,
Emotionally scarred, lost and stranded.
All his well-reasoned schemes, with no final coda,
Was dragged along against his will,
The double-standard, a puddle of metallic dross.

Why not let the cameras roll,
After all, he was pre-selected
To prop up the puppet regime
And blindly lead the blind pilgrims,
Catering to every pipe dream and every whim.
Nothing was really as it seemed.
None of it transpired in the way he expected.
When did it all get so painfully dull?
Then came the Exodus,
Forty years in the desert, wandering,
Following the rules etched in stone,

Pleading "set my people free,"
Just one step away from anarchy.
He was forced to climb the mountain all alone,
Bouncing obediently on the puppet string,
With wise counsel for the rest of us.

He never found the lost city of gold,
Nor anything of lasting adulation.
No visible scars won in battle,
Nothing to show, no Rubicon to cross,
His one-man crusade a near-total loss.
Mysterious inner voices now just prattle,
He yielded the sword of lofty expectation
To the young, the restless, and the bold.

44
WHO IS IN THE WATCHTOWER

The dark-haired girl came and burned the forest down.
Not a soul knew she was coming,
Creeping in from somewhere distant,
On quiet feet without a sound.
But as I tried to look the other way,
All around her the flames grew higher
And once again I had to learn
Where there is smoke there is fire.

Like the sirocco, she came and went
Leaving broken branches, broken hearts,
And an unkind reprimand.
Though destruction was never her intent
It was something I could never understand.
And though the wind portends a stormy, healing rain,
It was, at once, both my torment
And my unrelenting pain.

The young girl came and burned the aging forest,
Though the watchtower saw no sign of smoke,
We stood and watched as it burned before us.
The timber mourned, no one spoke
About the watchman absent from his post.
But we heard the ancient timber's lament--
The painful cry of the dying trees--
And counted what was lost.

Her dark eyes an unrelenting stare,
Black as the rock beneath our feet, and firm,
She looked us in the eye
And warned of her return.
She questioned every how or when or why--
A look on her face intimidated as she burned—
And we forgot what we had learned:
Courage appears to be in short supply.

The green-eyed beauty scorched the innocent forest,
And though she left behind a hundred clues
There would be no public trial, no arrest.
With evidence left behind, along the blackened floor
A world broken, ravaged, and torn.
In the traces of her footsteps
A billion seeds, released into a world reborn,
That the forest hadn't seen before.

The young girl came and burned the forest down,
Innocently at first, never asking how or why,
But with a lambent intensity in her eyes
That could pierce and punish and push mountains aside,
Or bring on smoky, darkened skies.
Unceremoniously escorted out of town,
Pushed along by a forceful western wind,
Her head held high, white linen robe un-blackened,
Calloused feet icy against the charred remains
Confident she would soon be back again.

45
PILGRIMAGE TO SAQQARA

I've been searching for honesty somewhere,
Behind your painted façade,
Hidden carefully in the darkest corners
Underneath a mountain of fraud.

But integrity comes in different hues
And different shades of rust,
A shadowy palette of self-righteousness,
And charlatans you can't trust.

   It's been a long, and painful journey,
   I'll be a long time gone I fear.
   This pilgrimage to Saqqara,
   And the ancient enlightenment here.

Scoundrels, convicts, and conmen
Selling snake oil and healing balms;
Gather round all you poor in spirit
Embraced in these heavenly arms.

Grab a shovel and a broom,
You'll get dirty here in the sty.
Pull on your pale green Wellies
And give honesty a try.

   It's been a long, and painful journey,
   I'll be a long time gone I fear.
   This pilgrimage to Saqqara,
   And the ancient enlightenment here.

High up on the mountaintop
Your sermons have been compelling.
Don't let truth stand in the way
Of the Kool Aid you've been selling.
Keep on preaching, keep on teaching;
Invoke charisma, poise and charm.
There are miracles to be witnessed;
Come and leave your generous alms.

It's been a long, and painful journey;
I'll be a long time gone I fear.
This pilgrimage to Saqqara,
And the ancient enlightenment here.

Come aunts and uncles, boys and girls,
Join the choir, raise your voice and sing.
The revival tent is open to anyone,
And we've got a cure for everything.

Come all you tattered and torn;
Your penniless, paupers and grievers;
Put your desperate hands up in the air
And cheer the true believers.

It's been a long, and painful journey;
I'll be a long time gone I fear.
This pilgrimage to Saqqara,
And the ancient enlightenment here.

It's a long, long journey home--
I may not ever come again.
The things that I've been searching for
Have been elusive in the end.

46
X MARKS THE SPOT

With a careless swagger, and a blissful glee,
He enters, glides, floats into any room,
Harboring a less-than-secret animosity--
Buried deep inside a lifelong gloom--
For everyone he touches, feels and sees.

He marches in as with a Sousa band,
A grand entrance with horns and drums and all,
And a written set of ill-defined demands
He posts with a nail on the windowless wall,
In a strange language no one understands.

Armed with a crossbow he takes his aim,
A lengthy list of reprimands--
Destructive, loud, and profane--
He makes his first defensive stand,
Looking for someone else to take the blame.

He doubted who he was, and all that he could be.
Like gears of a clock that don't engage,
The passage of time became an anomaly,
Quietly driving him to a ruinous rage,
And to the brink of stage-one insanity.

Never mind what you think you see--
Watch for hidden strings in the illusion--
It's a sloppy case of mistaken identity.

A lightening-fast sleight of hand and confusion,
And a tangled, twisted version of reality.

There was always a dose of courage and strength--
Small and carefully sequestered out of sight.
He could cleverly go to any length,
Ready to perform under stage lights--
A slick distraction from his very painful angst.

Now a toss of the coin in the air:
One side of the coin enigma:
Self-assured and uniquely debonair.
Bound in chains and social stigma:
The other side—the darkness of despair.

His emotional well had run nearly dry.
There was no logic, no clear reason,
Though he tried desperately to understand why
He had been a victim of treason,
Yet willingly agreed he'd been living a lie.

He could defy his critics and take a chance
On bold ideas; moving in a new direction.
He could courageously take an unpopular stance,
Or hide in dark shadows without detection,
Wallowing in the mud of victimhood and circumstance.

He's the only one who couldn't see
The light that burns deep in his soul.
The continual changes of his trajectory
Have long since taken a toll
On his innate confidence and bravery.

He carefully drew on lessons he'd been taught,
And found a map to a rich vein of gold,
And began to understand all the things he is not.
Take your compass, follow the map, he was told--
Just a little bit further, where X marks the spot.

Reluctantly, he agreed to stake a claim,
Emotionally drained and destitute.
Remembering that nothing, ever, stays the same,
Rewind clocks, reset, and reboot;
There are lost moments, lost time, yet to reclaim.

Keep digging, bring your pick, shovel, and pan__
There's gold down there, believe it.
Though it requires a different kind plan,
Over time, you'll successfully retrieve it.
If you stay the course, you can.

47
WHERE THE RIVER ENDS

I used to fish a small river--
More like a small creek I suppose—
That I shared with a dutiful osprey,
Or intruded on him shall I say.
Where the quiet has gone, no one knows.

My friend, the river, keeps an even pace
As she quenches, calms and cleans.
Though she is small, in the end
She joins with others as they wend
Their ancient road further downstream.

I've seen the grand estuary
Where the sea welcomes my friend, the river.
But now her weary, once vibrant eyes
Show only the tears she had cried,
Gone too, the love I tried to give her.

She arrives at sea, now a stranger,
So little of the shy girl remains.
The river that embraced me with her arms,
Now withered, her passion long gone,
She's been squeezed, diverted, dammed and drained.

Nothing left but a gentle murmur, perhaps, a sigh,
Crying gently in the dark of night,
The river is now un-navigable

The sins against her unforgiveable.
Where will the osprey and I reunite?

There's a new building blocking my view,
Soulless, with nothing to feel.
The architects will surely moan,
For the seeds they have sown,
Sprouting mausoleums of concrete and steel.

Where the vibrant river used to run,
The concrete is painfully out of place.
But dam up the rivers,
Make the parking lots bigger,
We never have quite enough space.

48
LIVING LIKE ROYALTY

You think you would like to live in a palace,
To hide away from all the citizens you abhor?
Or a castle with a drawbridge and moat,
With armed guards in full chain-mail armor?
And servants who, at the bell, come running
And then dismissed with the flick of a hand
From the private garden where you have been sunning,
Ready night or day awaiting your command,
With a biscuit and a cup of Darjeeling tea.
No wonder you want to live like royalty.

Some one to wake you up each day,
Wash your linens, make your bed,
And review your overburdened daily diary
Filled, mostly, with public appearances you dread.
So you cancel all that is obligatory--
There are much better things to do--
And you're awfully busy making history.
So, today, off to Zermatt to ski,
Hanging with the glitterati.
You could easily get used to living like royalty.
You could rule by simple caveat and dictate,
The whims of a ruler, no need for second opinions,
Intellectual thought, or serious debate.

No agenda, no reason, nothing more than caprice,
A fleeting fancy, a whim, a decree,
Motivated, perhaps by anger, paranoia,
Or jealousy. Or all three.
A despot who signs bogus laws with alacrity,
The right of the Noblesse oblige,
The temperamental choice of royalty.

You could choose to rule strictly by fear,
Use your heavy iron fist, command legions, roll heads.
This has worked for an array of tyrants over the years.
You could simply pass a law that demands respect and fealty,
Send in the black-cloaked honor guard
To enforce submission and unwavering loyalty.
Sign, in blood, the newly written manifesto.
No questions, no answers, the king wants it so,
Every facet a fait accompli.
Perhaps this is why you want to live like royalty.

Your face on every coin, every stamp, every bill,--
That sounds very heady and romantic.
Your name will be spoken reverently, yet harsh and shrill,
Your brilliant rule will be adjudged historic.
Everyone bowing down to your motorcade passing by,
This is the God-given right of a sovereign,
To decide which heads to roll-- who's out, who's in
And who may gaze upon your majesty.
The fragile, porcelain ego of royalty.

You could create new levels of palace chicanery,
A faulty pretense of governing, but in the end,
Just nonsense and never-ending malarkey.
Perhaps you like the idea of levying higher taxes,
There are, after all, your pet projects to fund,
Adding to the already heavy burden on the backs
Of the working and middle classes
Who bow en masse--and with a blind complicity--
To finance the unscrupulous charade
Of the badly overpaid, and unelected royalty.

As for me I'm reasonably comfortable,
Living in near poverty,
And bowing to no one, at least not any mortal being,
Who looks at me like his personal property
And expects me to kneel and kiss his gaudy ring.
Let me assure all, that I come proudly
From the wretched, humble masses
Where my lowly station allows me
To live free and embrace liberty,
My preferred version of royalty.

Ah, the royals, the royals,
Just look at them high in their royal towers
Around the world, across the seven seas,
Who cling to a peculiar brand of power
With perspicacity that allows them to see
What the rest of us peasants will never be able to see,
Leading us all to boredom, defeat, complacency,

No motivation to work, lethargy, lack of creativity,
And an undiagnosed, long running ennui,
Something never understood by pompous royalty.

The swagger and the arrogant rites of the endowed,
The chosen ones, those foreordained to rule,
Safely behind walls, away from the voices of the crowd,
Their right to govern by virtue of the correct gene pool.
You could send armies and legions to sow doubt and fear,
To wear the obscene crown, and occupy the throne,
With scepter in hand, and sword, mace, and spear.
Live in glass castles lined with golden filigree
That ornament the houses of the monarchy:
This may well be the strange attraction you have to royalty.

Maybe you like the idea of a crown on your head,
A bejeweled and ornamented clown hat
That attracts a string of mistresses to your bed.
Perhaps the allure is the naive thought
Of having nothing much to do except a little pageantry,
Dressed up and adorned with ribbons, medals, swords
Never won in battle, just a glimpse of shallow gallantry.
The birthright, never earned, only given,
Parading around pointlessly.
Ah the foolishness of ruling-class tomfoolery
Embraced by your favorite, local, royalty.

Dream about the regal life of the elite,
Demand a bow, a curtsy, a lowered head
From the vassals and everyone else you meet.
Every movement, every task, large or small

Becomes an event, a carefully arranged and scripted fete,
With caravans of horses, new and old-world pageantry,
Raised glasses, salutes, the obeisance of the masses
Will help you redefine and control the lower classes,
And continue looking down your noses, loathingly,
The way it's always been done by royalty.

Roll out the horse-drawn carriages,
Symbols, rituals, ancient rites,
Choosing only proper, pre-arranged marriages
Performed nightly under the lights.
Elegant couture and the latest in high-fashion,
Wallowing in mirror-image, all-consuming vanity.
Deliver speeches completely devoid of any passion
Reserved for the first in line, the heir to the throne,
The careful preservation of the aristocracy.
Is this what you expected from royalty?

It's easy to understand the appeal--
Not a bad gig, really, if you can get it.
So haughty, so sinister, and still so regal,
Maybe after a generation or two you'd chose to forget it,
Internalizing the disparity may make you regret it.
And it may end up different than you thought it would be,
So haunting, the constant glare, the constant stares
Of the unwashed, the lowly, the downtrodden,
People who may wish but never will be
Part of the bizarre world of the aristocracy.

Dear God, won't someone explain to me
The strange worship of earthly diety,

184 STILL THE RIVER FLOWS

The publicly sanctioned ruling class
Of aloof dummies we faithfully call royalty.
There's a new story but the same old cast--
You may have seen them recently--
An elite ruling class who cling to power at any cost,
Under a banner of democracy,
Claiming fraudulent elections where no one won or lost.
Staking permanent claims to the white throne,
As if it's something one man may, forever, own.
It's a clever ploy: change the rules, play a brand new game
And give absolute, unchecked authority a clever name.

Preserve this in your underground memoir,
The day you watched democracy die,
And we all bid our historic republic au revoir.
We thought we might give collectivism a try
And wound up with a dictator, a king, a powerful czar.
Beware the loss of liberty coming soon to a town near you.
Take a seat in the public gallery,
There's very little else for you to do.
Listen and watch as they re-define democracy,
Then pull up a chair and come and sit with me,
Share a cup of lukewarm Balmoral tea
And discover just how aloof, misguided, and shameless
The ruling class can be.

49
A CLEARING IN THE WOODS

There is a clearing in the woods
I stumbled upon quite innocently.
It's not something I was looking for,
I didn't find it, it found me.

Towering lodgepole pines surround it, this clearing,
Though no single shadow crosses as it should.
Permanently bathed in soft Rocky Mountain light,
This clearing in the woods.

Here is a spot, small, grassy, pristine.
Not a pinecone or a seed,
No evidence of footprints from man or beast,
Not a single broken branch or uninvited weed.

No scatological remains,
No bones or stones or detritus.
A modest patch of virginal mountain lupine
'Midst a grassy, dewy stillness.

Perhaps ancient druids came
And lovingly claimed it, cleared it.
An altar, perhaps a sacred shrine,
A reverent hush as I neared it.

Countless miles of Rocky Mountain timber,
A thousand acres, ten thousand more and then again,

Impossible to say where the tree line ends,
Or where the forest begins.

Trees fighting trees, brothers, cousins,
Siblings struggling, jostling for the right
To cast a shadow on this mysterious clearing,
Bathed in constant summer light.

It may be holy ground,
A silent voice worth hearing,
A path where only His feet passed
Through the reverence of the clearing.

It's dark here on the forest floor,
Cooler in the summer shade.
Shadows everywhere, shades of gray, dim,
The only light: the clearing heaven made.

A fear washed over me, a chill
As if the forest eyes were peering.
Then peace, enveloped by the haunting quiet
As I stood there in the clearing.

A million miles of trees and shadows
Somehow misunderstood
Their duty to shade this holy ground,
So, brightness shone upon the clearing in the woods.

Shadows lengthen as I turn away,
The end of day is nearing,
Forever haunted by the solitude,
And the reverence of the clearing.

I nodded, cast a backward glance
At this glade, this mead, this somber glen.
Homeward bound for a rest,
I doubt I'll pass this way again.

Sunrise hails a brand-new day,
Even as my end of days is nearing,
I journey on, stumble on, carry on,
Filled with the lessons of the clearing.

50

TAMAYURA

Best to gather up and walk,
No time to stand around and wait.
Your ship is never coming in,
Pack your bags and find a new place to begin,
But take note, the clocks are running late.

Pay attention to your dire circumstance,
How you ended up in this dismal state.
You've turned over every rock,
And diligently reset every clock,
An attempt to set the record straight.

Your youthful zeal is in the past,
Trailing far behind in your wake.
Chart a course for "what's next",
Ignore what everyone expects,
You'll get as much as you're willing to take.

The hourglass sand is nearly gone,
But you resisted taking the bait.
Understanding "Tamayura",
Did so little to reassure you,
Leaving just enough time to clean the slate.

So much adoration came and went,
So much drama on every page.
The budding debutante,

Has never known what she really wants,
With so little time up on the stage.

The script was laid on the table,
So you memorized chapter and verse.
The freak-show always seemed in fashion,
So you took the bet and tried to cash in,
If you just had more time to rehearse.

The aging clock again needs rewinding.
Something seems permanently stuck in the gears.
Let the pendulum swing.
Let the brassy bells ring.
Time has stopped, it appears.

Weathered playbills and photographs,
Evidence of a distant fame,
As reason tried to circumvent
And mute the artist's bleak lament,
Tamayura took all the blame.

You were caught looking at the clock
As the pressing deadline nears.
Your painful and private atonement,
Is measured in fleeting moments,
And calculated in falling tears.

The alarm by your bed has sounded,
For the third time today you hit snooze.
Afraid of self-inflicted pain,
There's still so much left to gain,
And, as it turns out, nothing much to lose.

There's a carefully crafted strategy,
Though some may see right through it.
Tamayura, tamayura,
Gave you such a short-lived bravura,
Recognized by those who always knew it.

Clinging desperately to might-have-beens;
To could'ves, maybes, and what ifs;
All the wishes and good intentions,
Didn't get much of your attention
While you perilously hung on to the cliff.

Courage, for years, has been retreating
Into darkest tombs and caves.
Not a moment of passion to waste.
Come into the light, make haste;
And see who's already dancing on your grave.

It's always been a tentative journey
That goes forward with or without you.
Moments you hoped would always exist,
Vanished somehow, into the gray, morning mist,
Then gone, blink, tamayura, right on cue.

*Tamayura (A short time or fleeting mome

51
SHOW ME A RIVER

Tell me a tale of a river,
Tell me what's around the next bend.
Tell me about its long, long journey
And how it's story ends.

Tell me about the meadows
And the flatlands it must traverse,
Or the canyons it must navigate
And how the water got there first.

Tell me of its rock-strewn paths
And how it wondered if it could survive
The first time it saw a canyon cliff
And made its first, daring dive.

Tell me of the travelers, the explorers, the pilgrims
Who leaned on the river's strong, guiding arm,
Who followed it on torturous summer days,
And bedded, at night, beside its peaceful, reassuring calm.

Take me, show me, lead me
So that I my see with my own eyes
Where the river first begins its life,
The home where it's humble soul resides.

I've stood beside a river,
I've fished the quiet mountain brook

But I knew not where to find the source of its power
Because I knew not where to look.

Show me where the mighty river goes,
Where it wends and bends and wanders.
Tell me the unwritten history,
It's humility, its majesty, its wonder.

Take me to the river that is always in a hurry
That rushes, dashes and frantically runs.
Go join it if that is what you choose,
Or come and sit with me beside the quiet ones.

Tell me why one river will angrily tell you,
With a scold, be on your way,
While others will lovingly grab your heart
and warmly bid you stay.

Tell me how the river charts its course
And chooses the direction it must flow,
To find its way across a thousand miles,
Help me understand how the river always knows.

Take me to the tiny, snow fed mountain stream,
And tell me about the river wide
That will require you to build a boat or a bridge
If you want to reach the other side.

Show me where the river runs,
But tell me first who decides
Which goes east and which goes west
From their home along the great divide.

Let me hear the voices of the rivers,
The ones that babble and bubble,
And rumble and tumble and thrash,
The ones that scurry, the ones that dally
And the ones that are always in a rush
Better still the ones that hush.

The humble one that whispers softly,
And the angry one that roars,
The one that say you're welcome here,
The jealous one that says not on my shores.
The modest voice, tender, soft and still,
The cleansing water, one who will always forgive,
And an arrogant river, the one who never will.

I've heard tell of rivers that grumble and growl and howl,
Wailing all night, their unrelenting moan.
Please take me to the quiet river,
Take me to the one with a reassuring tone,

And will utter, for me, a prayer of comfort
That I have never known.
How is it that one river is marron/brown,
Another blanca/white?
Why one river, by decree, runs cloudy
And, yet another reflects the light?

How is it that one river is verde/green,
Another is red/rojo?
One will nourish a vast, fertile plain,
The other flows where life refuses to grow.

One river lives forever in shadows,
Impossibly blind yet true,
While another lives in perpetual light
Reflecting the sky, the deepest azure blue.

A river is a recalcitrant child
Who roams and wanders aimlessly
And never finds his way back home
Because he doesn't listen, cannot see.

The river is a drowning man,
A broken spirit and a broken heart,
A confluence that brings us together,
Or a torrent that keeps us far apart,

Show me the rivers that run forever cloudy,
Others that run eternally crystal clear.
Please make sure it's a river that will speak to me
With an unmistaken voice that I can hear.

52
SMILES MAY CHEAT

Smiles will sometimes cheat,
But eyes will never lie,
And I can see in yours
A thousand reasons why.

Lips will turn and tempt,
And hearts will break, you'll see.
Love never comes neatly wrapped
In golden filigree.

Arms may caress, and warmly,
Legs are prone to run.
Ears may listen reluctantly,
Words may sometimes stun.

If she has a soul somewhere
I've tried but can't detect it.
There were glimpses of a passion,
But I failed to resurrect it.

Her exit was a planned escape
Which may have been foretold.
I decided not to follow her
As she stepped into the cold.

I did not trust her wicked smile,
The diabolical deceiver.
Her eyes have told me everything
That's why I can't believe her
Anymore.

Eyes will never lie to you
Though falling tears may take a toll.
They'll never cheat or lie to you,
But those eyes, those ice-blue eyes,
Those cunning eyes,
Are windows to her soul.

53
I HAVE A LITTLE SECRET

My best-kept secret is
That I have a well-kept, little secret,
All mine, one I've never shared.
(I've been nervous and scared.)
Some will want to know,
Others will never care
If I speak up
Or leave my soul completely bare.
No one knows,
Though I've put on a dazzling,
Highly entertaining show
Of amazing feats,
Labors, and losses,
Victories and defeats.

I carry it with me, this secret,
Every minute of every day,
And it follows me
As I come and go, leave and stay.
Coming home or running away.
I'm taking the secret with me
When I'm in my final abode--
Where no one can touch me,
Or persuade me; Or coerce me,

And guess what the secret might be.
As hard as they poke and probe--
I'll never reveal it--
Even as I depart
This giant, whirling globe.

My secret is nothing to be ashamed of,
No laws were ever broken,
No hateful words were ever spoken,
No judgments ever rendered,
No broken fences left un-mended
No lost sheep left untended,
No offense ever intended.
Yes, there were some oats I've sown--
Nothing others haven't done--
Yet no one has ever known.
While making the secret my very own,
The evidence shows just how much
My self-confidence has grown.

By finding inner strength to move along,
Courage has made me impenetrably strong.
There are painful lessons I have learned,
But they kept pushing me along.
Never being tempted
With a simple choice
Between right and wrong,
But, rather, thin and patchy fields of gray,
Such a wide array,
So many shades of gray,

So many dragons to slay,
So many wild imaginings
To choose from every day.

Friends would always call on me,
And they would come but never stay.
Perhaps it was my too keen intellect,
Perhaps my unblemished piety,
And how I kept my wildest,
Most dangerous impulses at bay.
I was always focused, driven,
And always had a clear direction,
A compass,
An inner guide,
A roadmap
That kept me comfortably
On the road to perfection.

The compass kept me from places
I should never go,
People I wouldn't want to know,
When to say "yes"
And how to comfortably say "no"
If I was to reflect the light
And forever keep my holy, inner glow.
No dark closets to purge,
No mournful, funeral dirge,
No rumors someone thought they heard,
No withheld evidence will ever emerge
That will keep me from my wings--
From soaring with the birds.

My closely guarded secret
Needs no guessing game.
I'm not revealing any names.
There are no prisoners to take,
No one else to share the blame,
No dirty hands or permanent stain.
Little anguish, very little pain.
I've waited at the station,
But never will again
Because I've already booked a seat
On the east-bound perfection train.
One small secret
Is all that remains.

There has never been
A single case of kiss and tell,
All relationships ended well,
No revolutions, no protests, no riot to quell,
No snake oil or phony potions to sell,
No petty crimes, no prison cell,
No headlines in the news,
No addictions, no vices,
No cuts, no scars, not a single bruise,
No wounded heart,
No battle scars,
Only steady guidance from my own,
Very private, North Star.

I've never had a drink of booze,
No drugs, no cigarettes,
No nightly hangovers,
Or morning after regrets,
No gambling, no games of chance,
No limitless bets.
No grand larceny,
No dirty tricks,
No chicanery.
Something in the way I was reared,
I didn't fret as vital deadlines appeared,
Didn't wait for a souvenir.
The judgment bar is something
I have never feared.

I'm neither a scoundrel nor a cheat,
A stowaway, a thief, or a dead beat.
I'm not running from the heat,
No hard drive to delete,
No parole officer to meet,
No homeless nights on the street.
But I do have a tiny, little secret
I'm still not ready to bury.
No uncertainty, no need to worry,
About the burden I may have to carry.
No verbal moans or exhalations
During the cross examination,
It'll take a little time
As both sides thrust and parry.

Look at me closely—
Clean and wholesome,
With character beyond reproach,
Still innocent, and so naive,
With grand expectations,
So badly flawed
Yet still so grandiose
As I make my final approach
From a painfully, long journey,
Places I've always wanted to see
On my trip to the place
Where I can, at last, get my wings.
Fill me with the light,
Let the heavenly choir sing.

But, before you find me,
Mercifully, innocent,
Before you pass your earthly judgment,
Before you close the circus tent,
Remind all who are still hell bent,
That I'm the one who's heaven sent.
Before you've all had your fill,
I have a well-kept secret,
That I'll keep hidden until—
Until all charges are dropped,
(I'll forget that you all hesitated)
When I am finally exonerated,
Until I'm fully forgiven,
And I pay the final bill.

There's never been a slanderous lie,
Not even the little white kind.
I've always turned the other cheek,
Kept an open mind,
And always did my best
To be fair and color blind.
But keep looking at my record,
The only thing you'll find
Is a roadmap to salvation,
And a lengthy dissertation
About my complete, total,
Unequivocal,
Undeniable and enviable
Peace of mind.

I've always kept the faith,
Read from the chiseled stone,
Ignored the pressure of the crowd,
Broken no commandments,
Lived life on my own, out loud.
I've contemplated the burning bush
By seeking to atone
For anyone who still desires
To throw the first stone.
I've followed the golden rule,
Joined the chorus of glad amens,
Eschewed violence and mayhem,
And always tried to make amends
With everyone--foe or friend.

Early on, I recognized the wild life,
Chose, rather, the mild life,
And kept my purity
Simple and child-like.
I've always sought forgiveness,
And made needed reparations,
Paid my dues and debts
And always offered generous oblations.
I preached the word, as I was told
To all the nations,
And raised a thunderous voice
With the distant congregations.
Coming to terms with the past,
Making whole what has heretofore been smashed.

I've screamed no epithets,
Hurled no insults,
Or pointed out others' defects.
You've seen how bullets deflect,
And how the light on me reflects.
I've never offered unjust criticism,
Spread no rumors,
Gossip or innuendo,
Believing you always reap
Exactly what you sow.
I've always given generously
So that my friends can plainly see
The depth of my humility.

Because my conscience
Is so clear and free,
(There is simply no one
Quite as pure as me.)
I've given up my parsimony,
Stood up to tyranny,
Patriotism came so naturally,
Settled differences effortlessly,
Fought against anarchy,
Written my last homily,
Tired of grappling with mortality,
Come join me in a somber reverie--
No need to light a candle--
To say three or four Hail Marys
Or take a knee.
There's not a single commandment
I didn't willingly obey,
No need for further contrition,
No excuses, no conditions,
And no need to pray.
I've put all childish things away,
Turned from the noise of the fray
Because the rapture could come any day,
And I'm ready to be swept away
With those of us, the chosen few,
Who have never wandered
From the straight and narrow way.

I call out to my captain,
"I am ready. On belay".

I doubt that I've forgotten
Or omitted a single thing.
I'm longing for the comfort
That only holiness can bring.
I've kept this one, small secret,
That I won't mention,
But it won't keep my ascension
From happening.
Poets will write about me
And choirs will surely sing.
Satan is sulking,
God is grinning,
Righteousness appears to be winning.

I've been pre-approved for salvation
Right from the very beginning.
Forget that I have a little secret,
Take a careful look at me.
Anyone will clearly see
There's not a single shred of vanity.
Heaven, surely, has an opening,
Open arms,
A welcome mat,
For someone just like me.

54
THE LAST BERRY ON THE VINE

Five or six, maybe more
Dying wasps, yellow jackets, hornets,
Didn't notice the "No Parking" sign
And huddled on a single blackberry,
Lying on the small puffy pillows
Of the ripe fruit, wearily supine,
Supping the deep, violet purple juice,
Here in my garden, on my decimated vines.

In July, the air-borne invaders arrived en masse,
Draining juice and life as if by evolutionary design,
A replacement for their long-spent nectar,
Celebrating, mourning,
Their fleeting life
Just one more time,
Leaving me, at season's end,
Not a single blackberry hanging on the vine.

September rust now colors the fronds,
Long, leggy, without a proper pruning.
The devastation of the bees, a felonious crime,
Left a thousand rock-hard berries,
Crusty nuggets, empty shells,
Forgotten, left behind,
Shriveled corpses, a sad remnant
Of the once vibrant blackberry vines.

The insects brazenly encamped through August
And declared it their own domain,
And dared a human hand to pick,
While frightened little girls stayed behind,
Politely declining bee stings and purple stains.
So, we come to the blackberries one more time,
Finding nothing, this September morning,
The season's end for the berries on the vine.

Wait, there is one last, fat, dark orb,
Hiding deep within the drooping fronds
Where I had to pull and push and peer
To find it tucked away from autumn sunshine,
Where the wasps can't find it.
The nectar gods tell me it is mine,
The very last of the chilly season,
The last blackberry hanging on the vine.

Because it was lost, forgotten, left alone,
This single berry grew and ripened in time,
Filled with summer sun and has grown
Into the largest of the season,
While all the others shrunk and withered.
The vineyard, now well past its prime,
Has left me this final nugget from the gold mine,
The last blackberry hanging on the vine.

Dark purple juices dot the muddy ground,

Evidence of thieves at the scene of the crime.

The fronds hang weary heads,

Anxious for their autumnal nap,

The days of frost not far behind,

A long, dark winter devoid of fresh fruit,

I savor this final bite, the nectar of the divine,

From this, the final blackberry hanging on the vine.

55
A MAN OF LITTLE MEANS

He's a man of little means,
And even less of real ambition.
It's a wonder he has any sense at all.
So it came as no surprise,
To see such darkness in his eyes,
And his precipitous rise and fall.

All his doubts were ponderous,
His questions came in waves
Along the road where all his wonder disappeared.
There would be no resolution,
Not even priestly absolution,
Could take him from the darkness that he feared.

Come and stay with me 'til morning
Here on this long, cool grass.
Come and stay until the darkness is gone.
It's not that I'm afraid,
If so, I wouldn't have stayed.
The answers that I need are just a con.

He wandered through the darkness,
With a billion stars to count,
And spent a thousand nights peering at the sky.
There was no illumination,
Just vapid hallucination,
As the stars sang their alien lullaby.

His steely eyes are weary,
As he stares into the void.
The answers should be coming any day.
He's alone and vainly wanting,
As the stars continue taunting
From more than a billion light years away.

Come and stay with me 'til morning
Here on this long, cool grass.
Come and stay until the darkness is gone.
It's not that I'm afraid,
If so, I would not have stayed.
The morning sunrise, now, is just beyond.

Leave the doubters where you found them,
You can make it on your own.
If there's a shadow of a doubt just hit re-send.
Those who would attack us,
On our personal road into Damascus,
Will find it a futile effort in the end.

Come and stay with me 'til morning
Here on this long, cool grass.
Come and stay until the darkness is gone.
It's not that I'm afraid,
If so, I would not have stayed.
The morning sunrise, now, is just beyond.

56
EYES OF ORNATA

There's a woman who, nightly, haunts my dreams,
And leaves not a footprint anywhere,
No evidence left at the crime scene,
No proof she was ever there.

She's as real as the darkness I live in,
Not just a fleeting, ghostly apparition.
She comes to me again and again,
Then silently slinks back to her sensual perdition.

She's got piercing eyes of Ornata,
The outlandish beauty of the Wildcat.
Her voice a hauntingly brief sonata,
Sung in the synagogue of her own habitat.

She's got the taste of trouble on her lips;
And her mouth says, "don't you dare".
I'm so naïve and poorly equipped,
To understand how little she really cares.

Her touch is soft as a feather,
Yet tough as chain-mail gloves.
I've had to keep my act together,
For an instant I thought I might be in love.

Her legs were built for coming and going—
She breezes in for a while, then gone—

Careless, wild, and all knowing
On the road, and far away by dawn.

Her silken hands, gently, caress my face,
Her fingers track traces of tears,
Her arms enfold me in a warm embrace,
Yet another trap, I fear.

She generously lends a listening ear,
But it turns out dangerously spurious,
Then vanishes, instantly, just as I feared,
Always emotionally penurious.

She's got the patient tone of a teacher,
Wise, gentle, and kind.
Heaven knows I've tried to reach her;
And explore her wickedly eccentric mind.

And all the rest of her,
Every square inch of her frame,
Every curve is ghostly and demure,
Every apparition ends exactly the same.

I begin my nightly quest for her,
In the corner near the shadow of doubt.
Just when I think I got the best of her,
Sunrise hands me a one-sided rout.

I've tried to sort the real from the fake,
But she's not at all what she seems.
I must keep myself wide-awake,
To keep her at bay from my nightly dreams.

I long for her to be honest, but she isn't?
How can I go on living this way?
How can anyone be more persistent?
How can I leave her? How can I possibly stay?

How can I possibly keep chasing her?
I've spent all my emotional wealth.
How can I possibly keep pace with her?
This can't be good for my mental health.

She's a little bit rich, but insists she's poor,
A little bit tender, a little bit tough,
Always wanting, always taking more,
Giving her everything is never enough.

Put all the pieces together,
Roll it, neatly, into one ball,
Careful, the game goes on forever,
Because she has no heart at all.

There's a girl who, nightly, haunts my dreams,
And leaves not a footprint anywhere,
No evidence left at the crime scene,
No evidence she ever cared.

The dawn-colored brain fog dissipates,
I'm ready to move on, and to heal.
I've learned painful lessons far too late;
Turns out she's very much alive, and painfully real.

57
INTO THIN AIR

Somewhere between the ceiling and the sky,
There is a space,
A place,
Where dreams go to evaporate,
And wishes go to die.

It's the thin air above us, distant as a star,
A billion light years,
A million tears,
Where prayers seemingly vanish
Having traveled so far.

Who is listening to each plea, every cry,
Our greatest fear?
There's no one here,
Where doubters are welcome
And people of faith need not apply.

Gone the apparitions on the road to Damascus,
An answered prayer
Here and there,
A random blessing, perhaps,
But nothing for the rest of us.

There are no more visions,
We've lost our faith, lost our soul.
A new level of doubt has taken a toll.

People of faith long ago perished
Leaving them no place to go.

On the altar of good taste,
Reputations dragged,
Faithful voices gagged,
And virtue has been sacrificed
In the graveyard of the chaste.

No voice, no prophet, no Oz,
Philosophers are under attack,
Virtue isn't coming back,
With no sage, no oracle, no shaman,
Redemption, sadly, is a lost cause.

In vain we search for kingly mansions on high.
The streets of gold,
We've long been told
Are within our human grasp--
A weary, ancient lie.

We send anxious pleadings heavenward
And wait for a reply,
And try
To hear the faint whisper,
Piercing, a dog whistle, mostly unheard.

All hope has passed us by,
The circus parade,
The big charade.
Seeds of doubt scatter in the restless wind,
Gone in the twinkling of an eye.

It has become increasingly clear,
The only voice you hear
Teaches a devilish fear
That has closed all believing ears,
Leaving a gash in the atmosphere.

Faith and hope are under attack.
Manna for the famished,
Miracles have vanished
Into thin air, doubtful
They are ever coming back.

58
SOMETHING SHINY

You seem anxious, a little distraught,
Your brain tangled in twisted knots,
Unable to recall anything of value you were ever taught,
       And what you really need to know.

All that mattered came from the street,
Finding out education is so incomplete,
Keep moving to the unfamiliar beat
       As onward, onward you go.

Walk in lock step, no regrets,
Placing irresponsible, long shot bets.
Nothing to remember, very little to forget,
       It's so much easier that way.

My, my how your choices were pre-selected,
Packed in egg cartons, safely protected,
Ruled by passions mostly undetected,
       So you turn, turn and walk away.

Something shiny, something dull,
Tested in the unforgiving crucible,
Brand the calf and castrate the bull,
       Then tell them you're a cowboy.

Never one to slash and burn,
Looks like you narrowly missed your turn

To put your ashes in an Asian urn.

What a clever boy, clever ploy.

Turns out you're easily persuaded,

Believing you may have finally made it.

Cut your losses, sell it, trade it

Before the sand runs out.

Turn up the lights and use high beams,

To illuminate the smoky scenes

That share a border with the obscene.

No clue what they're about.

Isotopes and ends of ropes,

Using all the familiar tropes

To hide your dreams and shattered hopes,

And write your mysterious screenplay.

Listen carefully to the rules,

They've prepared your standard set of tools.

You'll never again have to suffer fools

If you do exactly what they say.

Roller coasters and hippie vans,

A sorry little rock and roll band,

A frail alliance of also-rans

Who just wanted to put on a show.

Trophy wives and butcher knives,

You may have used six of your nine lives,

Leaving you battered and barely alive.

Make sure everyone knows.

Hollyhocks and peacocks,
Dilapidated city blocks,
Unwound antique Grandfather clocks.
    Make passing time elusive.

Shaved ice, roll the dice,
The twisted logic made you think twice,
Took the deal and paid the price
    Though the numbers were inconclusive.

Mothballs and painted walls,
Making sense of angry scrawls,
Staying clear of barroom brawls
    And indelible black ink.

Red cliffs and monoliths,
Overtime and second shifts,
Too many maybes and what ifs
    Left you teetering on the brink.

Empty halls and creepy dolls,
Empty boxes in dying malls,
Erecting short-term border walls,
    To keep out the great deceiver.

Just a bit past your prime,
You ran the marathon in record time,
But left the part-time farm girl gentle on your mind.
    And became a conscientious, wary believer.

Nights were tilted, hopes all wilted,
Thrice in one week abandoned and jilted.
A classic case of "he said/she said."
    And the jury, in the end, was hung.

Here's the undisputed leader
Confessing, publicly, he no longer needs her.
The diamond princess wrapped in fur
       Vanished as the final hymn was sung.

Victory had at last been won,
Though the desperate fighting had just begun,
As if in a black and white TV re-run,
       Drowning in quicksand and swirling pools.

You're poised to go far, very far.
Treated like a pulp-fiction super-star,
As long as you're willing to lower the bar
       And arbitrarily change the rules.

Come and meet me at the equator,
We all end up in the middle sooner or later,
Branded as an undercover spy and traitor
       Just seeking some middle ground.

Everything, you assume, will be just fine,
As long as you don't cross the Maginot line
Running between ridiculous and sublime,
       Separating what is lost and what is found.

You'll hear the whispers, an idle boast,
The sanctimonious prayer of the genial host,
With his newly painted whipping post,
       His leaky schooner run aground.

In his hand, the newly minted manifesto,
A long forgotten Barnum side show,
With vague intentions bathed in shadow,
       His pulpit, an ancient burial mound.

Too much time spent in a bread line
Questioning what's yours and what's mine.
Sort the messy recyclables one last time
       And expose the embarrassing charade.

There are massive breeches of decorum,
Beyond debate in any forum,
But don't cast a vote without a quorum
Of the obsolescence brigade.

Ethics out the window and hanging on the line,
Honesty and integrity are in steep decline.
Step across the Mason Dixon line
       And call it victory.

It's politics and policy of anesthesia.
Say what you want, no one will believe ya.
Run back home and tell your pa,
       Trust me, he'll agree.

Searching for gold in California,
Before I come I'll be sure to warn ya,
But take your time and let the legions adorn ya
       And set you apart from the status quo.

You've taken the worst of ridicule and scorn,
Devoted to the cause but still emotionally torn,
You took a vow, now saved and newly reborn.
       Stand back and polish the halo.

Pompoms and escalators,
Afro hair and agitators,
Call in the professional negotiators
       To diffuse the lethal bombs.

Leave the nest and head due west.

Don't make anyone second-guess.

No matter the question always say yes.

      You're now at home, where you belong.

Eggnog and catalogues,

Across the street, avoid the dogs,

Keep your secrets shrouded in fog

      And don't forget to fill the moat.

Racing bikes and labor strikes,

Rocky trails and steep mountain hikes,

Tell me whom you really like,

      And don't forget to vote.

Trying to make the hit parade,

Admitting it's a massive masquerade.

All the earth-toned costumes tailor made

      For the premiere of the righteous revolution.

Sacred vows and sacred rites

Long forgotten on Saturday nights,

With a blurred line between wrong and right,

      There'll be no absolution.

Baptism and circumcision,

Up on the big screen in Panavision,

It's the sparkling new millennial religion

      Of the perplexing digital age.

Missionaries, mercenaries,

Trial balloons and coal mine canaries,

Winged angels and glittering fairies

      Dancing on the world's biggest stage.

You've changed your stripes and course corrected,

Lighted candles and genuflected,

Your humble confessions were undetected,

> So disregard what the critics are saying.

Peering through the kaleidoscope,

Taking little blue pills to help you cope,

Now's not the time to give up hope,

> But, please, for heaven's sake, keep on praying.

French cuisine and Cuban cigars,

Autographs of superstars,

Broken bones and unsightly scars,

> With no one left to trust.

Kings, Princes, and Russian Czars,

Ride precariously on my handlebars,

With gazing eyes on distant stars,

> Disappearing into rust.

Cracker jacks and mustache wax,

Fending off another heart attack,

Resolved to move forward, never back,

> With a galling dearth of choices.

Red doors painted black,

Leave them open just a crack,

Out of tune and badly out of whack,

> Those chilly, ancient voices.

Dump trucks and concrete,

Fall asleep and wreck the fleet,

Suddenly one career is incomplete,

> Still time to find another.

Scrupulously avoiding censure,
You settled on stricter measures,
Supplementing guilty pleasures,
        The ones, foretold, that take you further.

Hill climbs, hard to finds,
Break some rules, ignore the signs,
Complex teachings by design,
        Never mind, don't bother.

Alphabets, guitar frets,
Broken hearts you still regret,
Your excuses still seem circumspect,
        Explain them to your biographer.

Boldly seize the stage, forget the clouds,
Turn up the music, ignite the crowd,
Sing it joyfully. Sing it loud,
        But be certain you've turned on the mic.

Arbitrage and sabotage,
Groupies and cling-ons in your entourage
Came wrapped in patriotic camouflage
        Where everyone looks exactly alike.

Moral choices, doctored books,
Altered reality, and second looks,
Hoist a flag and see what works
        For the raspy, vox populi.

Rev up the hand painted tour bus,
Listen for the distant chorus,
Sung by those who've gone before us,
        Waving the tattered flag as you go by.

Hidden meanings, careful gleaning,
Remind me once more which way you're leaning.
Your clever lines obscure the deeper meaning,
          Acknowledging you can't have it both ways.

Left with little room but to agree,
Send secret messages no one else can see,
Crafted with unpleasant pedantry,
          That's just the way it's done these days.

Brown shoes and bad news,
Feeling like you've forever been abused,
Stranded on a dry-dock cruise
With no sextant to guide you home.

Rooms full of straight-backed pews,
With only simpletons left to amuse,
Learning to tolerate radical views,
          As hearts begin to turn to stone.

So many public defenders to accuse,
Innocent bystanders to abuse,
Cynicism still your only muse
          As you plan a massive sit in.

Organ pipes and teletypes,
Trying to avoid the hollow hype,
Call me when the cherries are ripe
          And we'll come and help you pit 'em.

Where the river wends,
Concrete begins and asphalt ends,
If you can't be honest, simply pretend
          You have all the answers.

Working late, celebrate,

Choking on unnatural hate,

So many new worlds to circumnavigate.

       If you can't, no one can sir.

Broken skis and broken knees,

Leave the pack, do what you please,

Dissent always comes with such ease.

       Make sure you cover your tracks.

Lemonade in Pepsi cups,

Avoid the guards and drink it up.

Steady on you untrained pups,

       And always check your back.

In the end, a solitary man,

In the end, a black sedan,

In the end, just another also ran

       And, oddly, a new beginning.

Mend a fence, make recompense,

Mount your lengthy self-defense,

Speak quietly, clearly in the present tense,

       The final out, the final inning.

59
ACROSS THE GREAT DIVIDE

You and I are far apart
And it feels at times we're ready,
Longing,
Starving,
For a fresh start,
Our differences carefully measured,
Metered, ignored.
Time to move on,
Move up, move out,
Move along and cut the cord.
All frustrations and resentment,
Insistently, held inside,
Finally came flowing out,
We let them out.
And now we'll walk away without direction.
We'll let the wind decide.

For far too many years
I've been heading due west,
And you are moving,
Creeping slowly, to the east,
With or without your usual fears.
And I don't know up from down,
In from out,

Coming or going,

The chasm, deeper than it is wide,

Pulled by the whims of nature

Across the continental divide.

Remember when we found the headwaters,

Where the starlings hide,

The heron's nest,

Berries on the hillside,

And when the Indian paintbrush blooms.

Remind me when the south wind blows

And how we always swam against the tide.

I'll miss you,

Especially the thought of you.

A flood of memories, a torrent

That washes me, strengthens me,

And, gently, helps me take my loss in stride.

As you leave

I'll count the sunsets you missed,

And with vacuous eyes

Remained distant, preoccupied.

I will give you an assist,

Point you in the right direction,

But I won't give you a ride

Through the forest in autumn

As you crash the wedding

Of a September bride.

Lost in the woods you shrunk,

Became a claustrophobe,

The trees a prison,
Locked you away,
Far, far away
From open skies
Too dense to see,
Too dark to see,
The quiet woods, once your friend,
Now a spiteful enemy.
But it's not your place to choose
Not your job to decide,
To clear cut the trees--
A vengeful act of forest genocide.
Recall that this was our cathedral,
The temple of black lava rock,
The steeple a lodgepole pine,
An impenetrable wall,
A fortress,
Far, far away,
Safely away from hypocrisy,
Away from idle chatter
Where piety and sanctimony
Are the only things that matter.
Out here silence will do just fine.
The alters where we worshipped,
The saints we beatified,
Are away,
Far, far away
Where we can't hear the tongues wag,
Or hear the self-righteous brag,

Where truth has just one side,
Where arrows sling,
And pious words deride.
We were at peace here--
We thought we were at peace here--
We hoped we had peace,
Proud to be counted
As dissidents, resisters, loners,
Misfits, misbehaved and wild eyed.
Then came the avalanche,
Then came the earthquake,
Then came a flood,
Unleashing a rockslide
Of animosity,
Hurtling insults and unkind words,
Flying debris,
Leaving a swath
More than ten miles wide.

Recall when we were dodging bullets
And taking bets on the side.
I was the one who held you up,
Wrapped a blanket around you,
Held you closely
as you shivered in the cold and cried.
Cried for the peasants,
Cried for the kings,
Cried for the riches that we never had,
And the futile chase

Of the elusive brass ring.

Recall the scene for me

When all the horses died,

And you went underground

Hiding, alone,

Betrayed and petrified,

Trembling, terrified

That you'd be found to be the killer.

I believed you, I stood by you

Until you found your footing,

Until you once again hit your stride.

But you stayed away,

Far, far away,

Lost and wandering for a season,

You lost your hope,

Lost your sanity,

Lost all reason.

I clung to your promise,

Still I believed you would return to me.

But ominous clouds

Covered the north star,

Traveling treacherous routes

Without a guide,

Trusting you to come back home,

Take up your earthen bed

And once again sleep by my side.

I trusted that you'd remember

The lesson of the woods,

That moss grows only on the north side

Where it's shady and cool,

Where there is only filtered light.

Follow the moss if not the stars,

Follow light and shadow, lose the pride.

Oh the earth's scent,

Oh the colors that are heaven sent,

Oh the uncharted roads we tried,

Oh the soles of walking shoes

That left minute particles of our pain,

Grains of our honest aspirations

Callously tossed aside.

But now,

After we agreed to go in new directions,

Different directions,

Separate directions,

Walk don't run.

There was, in the end,

Very little pain,

But still you claimed victory,

Your race was won.

You were lauded,

You were applauded,

All feelings disregarded.

Your heartless reaction

So predictable, so Pavlovian,

Walking away is finally

Something we can agree on,

No chance to begin again.

The long, summer days are gone.

Autumn paints the skies the color of freedom,

A final, peaceful rest at eventide,

Grass and pine boughs

A pillow for your head.

Look heavenward, say a prayer of thanks,

And gleefully wallow in your pride.

60
A BOX ON THE WALL

I've been looking for a new identity,
But all the choices look the same.
When my unstable symptoms at last abate,
I'll attempt to set the record straight,
And finally clear my good name.

I've seen a stranger's face in the mirror,
As well in the precinct files.
The public defender
Won't let me surrender—
Confessions are suddenly so out of style.

It's simply not my face in the mirror,
It's a haunted ghost staring back.
It's a painful, agonizing view,
From inside the "most-wanted" milieu,
And the waning self-confidence I lack.

I've tried to ignore all the terror
Behind the glassy stare.
My disposable, cheap disguise
Barely covers up the mounting pile of lies.
This convict is going nowhere.

Clinging onto the faraway youthful era
While holding back my immature rage

Desperately hanging from vapors
And the burden of heavy labor,
Trying to reconcile this high-def visage.

I don't look a thing like I'd hoped,
The changes that my ignorance wrought.
So many strictures to obey,
Then arrogance got in the way,
And the unshakeable loathing has all been self-taught.

There's a troubling darkness and a horror,
When I've had the courage to stare.
I've willingly taken all the blame,
And forgiven everyone who came
Looking for the missing person in there.

Sad eyes are looking back at me,
Sad heart has gone M.I.A.
I've tried diligently to explain
The headwaters of all the pain,
But no words of comfort are left to say.

Compulsively gazing into the mirror,
Searching vainly for a single clue,
Getting my bearings straight,
My carefully planned departure can't wait
For an intimate, oft delayed rendezvous.

The withered and aging face
Is trapped inside a box on the wall.
The tragicom countenance,
Completely devoid of common sense,
Awaits its final curtain call.

Probing and peering deeper for insights,
So many words left unspoken.
The mirror right in front of me,
Goes on and on into eternity,
And the circle of life is never broken.

The mirror is always honest and candid
With the mournful soul looking back.
Never any deceit, never any lies,
No where to run, nowhere to hide,
Just undiluted evidence and facts.

The mirror never asks how you're feeling,
Never queries, "how's your day" or "where've you been?"
The mirror simply reflects,
Doesn't remember, but never forgets,
And gives back only what you put in.
Once mounted and hung above the sink,
The mirror keeps its silent vigil.
Whether chipped, cracked, faded or bent,
There are no facts or laws to circumvent.
It's always truthful and hanging there still.

As you daily remodel yourself in the mirror,
Many versions of you have come and gone.
The mirror's annual report,
Judged by the vanity circuit court,
Is always right, yet, regretfully very wrong.

It's possible the mirror is your best friend,
Yet frequently leaves you abandoned.
Its message is elemental,

Its wisdom fundamental,
And self-pity and envy are banned.

The reflection is quiet and shy,
Never speaks, yet so wise and so clear.
You have always feared it,
Though you never hear it
Teaching you what you most need to hear.

61
MEET ME AT THE VINE

Come little one,
Sit here for a moment at my side
And tell me again
Why you don't come to pick berries
In my garden anymore.
Or the apples, or the plums,
Or dig for carrots.
Tell me the berries are all gone,
Remind me it is October
And the fruit is past its prime.
Tell me you forgot,
Tell me you don't want purple fingers,
Tell me you are afraid of bees,
But please don't tell me
You ran out of time.
It is late Autumn, I'm cold,
And my hands are purple stained.
I'm the one who is short on time.
Come little one,
Meet me at the vine.

Come little one,
Come close but don't stand
On my brittle toes

Like you did when we danced
And our feet moved together,
Yours on top of mine.
Dance again with me little one.
Tell me you've forgotten the steps,
Tell me you've lost the music,
Tell me your feet don't move
Like they used to, that's just fine.
Tell me you've lost the beat,
But please don't tell me you have no time.
It is I who can't move my feet,
I'm the one who has lost the music,
Lost the rhythm, lost the beat.
Come little one, be patient and kind,
Let's dance again with our feet intertwined,
Find the forgotten steps.
I'm the one who has so little time.

Come little one
And paint a picture with me.
Don't worry about the mess,
Paint recklessly outside the lines.
Come paint my portrait
Like you used to
When I had curly hair
And my eyes were bright.
Tell me you can't remember the colors,
Tell me you can't find pen and ink,
Or a sheet of paper, or a brush.

But please don't tell me
You can't paint a silly picture
Because you haven't the time.
Slow down, why the rush?
I have watercolors, I have paper,
I have a palette and a brush.
Come paint with me while the sun still shines.
I'm the one who has lost bright eyes,
And I'm the one who is running out of time.

Come little one
And show me how you tumbled, bounced,
Flipped, and jumped, and twirled,
And never stopped moving--
My upside-down girl.
Let me see again your effortlessness,
Your graceful hands, strong arms,
Your courage and fearlessness.
Tell me you've lost your strength,
Tell me that your feet hurt,
That you've lost your youthful restlessness.
Tell me bending over backward
Was something done in other days.
But please, little one, don't say you haven't the time
For a twirl, a final pirouette.
I'm the one who has lost my strength,
Lost most of my regrets,
But haven't yet, lost my mind.
I am the one whose back won't bend,
And I'm the one who is running out of time.

Come little one
And sing another song for me,
One about the princess who is lost--
It was always a princess lost--
And you knew every word,
Sung loud as if you're the one
The prince had saved.
Sing it again for me.
Tell me you've forgotten a few words,
Tell me you've forgotten the rhyme,
Tell me your voice is faint,
But please don't say you haven't the time
To once again, sing for me.
I'm the one with lost voice, lost rhyme.
So come, little one, this cold October day.
I have so little time, I fear.
Frost is on the berry vines,
And all the fruit is gone.
Come little one, come sing of princesses
Just one more time.

62
THE PRINCELY CROWN

It's eleven-fifteen
And here am I, the prince of clowns,
Making my way, at last
To the blurred edges
Of this dirty, God-forsaken town.

Banished from the kingdom of fools
I abdicate my princely crown,
Against my will, against the rules.
A brief stay atop the throne,
Over before it began.

At eleven-twenty
I mount the weary, swayback brown,
Aboard the saddle, backwards
I see things from an enlightened perspective.
No need to turn around.

Lights in the harbor have dimmed,
Reluctance the only sound.
A pandemic of malaise arrived on cue,
And a lengthy, emotional drought
Has run the ships aground.

It's eleven-forty-five,
I'm tired of chains, duty bound.

The glaring lack of normalcy
Is difficult to explain,
Impossible to understand.

A drought of despair washes in,
Flattening earthen mounds,
Laying bare the rocky shores,
Leaving parched and scorched
This once fertile ground.

At eleven fifty-five
Supplicants post their demands
Then disappear into the dark.
A crafty legerdemain,
A cowardly sleight of hand.

One minute before midnight,
The clocks will not be rewound.
Close your eyes, your ears,
Come, one last time, stroll with me
Around the hallowed grounds.

The midnight peals ring out
Their hollow, unforgiving sound.
Prussian-blue shadows paint the wall,
And all the lemmings have retreated,
Safely underground.

Time and space have withered,
Down is now up, up is now down.
Wandering aimlessly without a map,
Getting hopelessly lost, it appears,
Is the surest way to be found.

Twelve-O'one, a new day,

The guests have all left town.

A desperate bride clings to the altar,

Alone in her tattered,

And threadbare wedding gown.

The wedding cake has melted,

The minister is nowhere to be found.

No one is saved by the bell, saved from hell,

Gone the robes, gone the gloves,

A knockout in the final round.

63
INTO THE MIST

Dawn came heavy again today,
A bleak rain, a blanket of mist.
I stepped into the gray morning,
Uneasy about what may lie ahead,
Terrified of all the things I may have missed.
A gauzy apparition with hollow eyes, appeared--
Eyes of glass, viridian blue--
Dangerous to stare, too haunting to resist.
A tarnished amulet hung 'round her neck,
A wilted orchid tied upon her frail wrist,
And when the faint music stopped
The road took an unexpected twist
that I could not have seen coming.
Desperately I tried to look away,
But disaster is always impossible to resist.
She bade me follow her down corridors of gray,
Distant voices wailing, warning,
"This may be the end," they all insist.
But I've heard it all before,
Seen a thousand gray days like this.
Then, as I arrogantly probed the edges of doubt--
Dire warnings far too easily dismissed--
I slipped into the blackness,
From the precarious edge of jagged cliffs,

Desperately clinging to a brittle branch
Others must have missed,
Then felt her bony, white hand reach out
And pull me back from the dank abyss.
Quietly, I thanked her, then walked away,
But still the wounds are painful,
Still the scars of doubt persist,
My deepest longings so much different
Than a prayer or any ordinary wish.
As I count the times I confidently stood my post,
Bathed in fragrant overconfidence,
As well, the many times I demurred,
And wallowed in the stench of cowardice,
I think of the countless times
I was warmly welcomed home,
Yet felt, at times, that I was never missed.
There are fewer things, now, to remember or forget,
But even fewer things I'll miss.
Solemn days, heavy, gray days linger,
But nothing quite as painful as this.

64
ROTTING PUMPKINS

Get off your high horse my friend,
Come down from the lofty tower
Where you learned your phony ways
And your arrogance always so well-rehearsed.

Deftly you put on quite a show.
Quite a practiced actor, it turns out.
Your secret is safe, there is little doubt
Both of us are uncomfortable with truth.

The small print of your guaranteed contract
Was always difficult to understand--
Nothing beyond the paper and ink
Was of any measurable worth.

Promises, you learned, are frequently violated,
With neither remorse nor visible angst.
Your passion is highly overrated,
And sorrow, as always, is such a weak excuse.

Your hard, square edges defined you,
Exactness your daily quest,
And though your best days are behind you now
You remain insistently obtuse.

But, pre-packaged promises turned out to be
Cinderella pumpkins rotting in the field,

And your glass-slipper elegy
Was just a well-executed ruse.
There's a newly built tower waiting for you,
A new flight of stairs to climb.
Come up straightaway and place around your neck
The sturdy hangman's noose.

65
COVERED IN DUST

It's a dismal end of another chapfallen, January day.
The bright, clear, hoar frost has disappeared,
The trees and your factory clothes
Are a dingy, stone-washed gray.
The air is dirty, so too your lungs,
The sky, your options, your mood and your steel toed boots
Are all colored in a deep patina of rust.

Darkness fell this night with a dull thud,
As street lamps struggled, sputtered,
To cast their anemic, bluish glow,
Reflected in the thick carpet of winter mud
That came with an intermittent thaw,
Revulsion covering the ground in
An indecipherable texture of dust.

Friends, like birds, have taken winter flight.
There is no one here to warm your empty chair,
Or dine on your emotions,
Or warm your bed this January night.
No one to count the endless minutes,
No one to exculpate your torments,
No one left to trust.

No one to help paint your sidewalk art
With confusing shades of cloudy pastels
That all run together when it rains,
And you can't finish because you don't know where to start.
Gray looks like blue, yellow appears green,
And there are no knobs to endlessly twist and turn,
No antiquated color balance to adjust.

With frozen feet, your journey, oft delayed,
Charted with a map, now sadly out of date,
Your tragic shoes badly worn,
Your jacket and your optimism badly frayed.
Your loner's path never included me,
Not what we both hoped for,
Not what we planned, not what we discussed.

It was a desperate, desolate wanderlust,
Insulated by the choices you made,
The things you alone set out to do,
Disregarding what others said you must,
Then quietly, aimlessly wandered away
Into a quantum of misery and an overabundance
Of self-loathing and impermeable disgust.

66
THE STARS WE SLEPT UNDER

Come sit with me and celebrate
All the star-lit skies we slept under,
Constellations that filled our eyes,
Every drop of rain, every cloud a wonder,
Every flash of lightning,
Every distant clap of thunder.

The endless, carefree days we'd explore
Places we had never been before,
So many far-off lands yet to plunder,
So many fences to climb over,
Or, on bellies slide under
And see what's on the other side.

So many kingdoms to put asunder,
Castles to storm, flags to surrender,
Leaning on ignorance and raw courage,
Learning from broken bones, broken hearts,
Every accidental fall, every blunder,
And the billion tears we cried.

Celebrate with me the girl who haunted my dreams,
A portrait in sepia tones and burnt umber,
For countless hours I'd hunt her,
Then missed the day she called my number
While I was buried deep in the innocence
Of a youthful, worry-free slumber.

Come celebrate all the rivers we ran,
Uncharted waters we sailed, rocky trails we explored,
The rules we broke or blissfully ignored,
Battles waged with wooden swords,
Building our forever fortresses
From someone else's discarded boards.

The races we won, the touchdowns we scored,
Historians, in dusty books will record
We thought of neither consequences nor rewards--
Sometimes fueled by bravery,
More often lost in bone-headed naïveté,
Our victory song in minor chords.

It's my time, now, for looking backwards,
A time for looking heavenward,
A time to boast of confidence and bravery,
And confess, as well, the times when I was a coward,
Each step now a burden of weighted legs,
But patiently, hopefully, still moving forward.

There are so many mountains yet to cross,
So many white-water rivers yet to ford,
The glasses now are polished clean,
The final wine is poured,
As we remember when our voices barely whispered,
And celebrate the times they roared.

67

THE ABYSS

Look into the abyss,
The empty cavern where my heart used to beat.
Take your time, there are details you may have missed.
Don't be afraid of what you'll find.
The rhythm has changed
And you'll discover there is a
Passion of a different kind.

Look deeply at the creases in my face,
Weathered and worn,
Deep and hollow spaces.
Take your time and follow the map
The lines have drawn, a painful place
Down a deserted, desolation highway,
That time and sorrow cannot erase.

Look into my eyes, deeper than before,
And find the playfulness,
There, just behind the blind spot,
The center of mischievousness
That allowed us to be brave, daring,
To eschew all seriousness, sorrow now in our past,
Scarred, scared, yet victimless.

Our history, our story, now revisionist.

Feel free to exaggerate the tales,

Add partly-true details if you wish.

Our past is now our present

Tangled up with complicated worries

As our doubts get bigger

And our fears persist.

Our love affair was filled with turns and awkward twists,

And we finally turned our backs and walked away

With neither a final verdict nor a final kiss.

The taste of you hung on heavy hearts

As we made a vow to seal our lips,

And, unless in reverent tones,

To never again speak of this.

You, the hopeful one, me the pessimist.

You danced on air--clouds your stage--

With an effortless grace no one could resist.

Me with a temper, pushing people off the cloud

With clenched jaw and iron fist.

Not the man you dreamed of,

Not what you imagined, not exactly what you wished.

Look into the depths of my soul, so much is amiss,

Barren now, hollow, empty

Searing pain not easy to dismiss.

Down the stairs to the dank cellar

Where rows of dusty, blue-tinted mason jars

Have preserved forever the misery

Of our cob-webbed, long-abandoned tryst.

Peer through my darkened, muddy windows.
Come in from the cold and get warm.
Sit with me and count the moments of our cowardice
Measured against all the double-dog dares,
A faded, pastel shade of bliss.
Thankfully, no one is counting,
Sadly, no one really cares.

Look at me now, a rusted car propped up on blocks,
That others say can never be fixed.
A hollow, empty shell, too far gone,
"But we must try," you would insist.
So much rust, we didn't know where to start,
Reminding me how you could put me back together,
As well the countless times I fell completely apart.

68
DAVID'S HARP

You sang to me in dulcet tones,
In minor keys a mournful song,
And here with you I'm so alone,
Your heart is not where I belong.

I heard your voice, as if by chance,
And then you sang as if a prayer.
I cannot change my circumstance,
Or find an answer anywhere.

So, if your voice was heaven sent,
A healing balm from David's harp,
You won't forgive, I can't repent,
Nowhere to end, no place to start.

The choir sings adagio
And on the air the bells will peal.
But still, I have no place to go,
And this broken heart will never heal.

Come sing for me just one more time,
And hear again your sad lament,
Forgotten chords, a haunting rhyme,
The story how you came then went.

You lifted me to sacred heights,
Then left me here on bended knee.
Please stay and sing with me tonight
The song that always comforts me.

The light is gone, the dark descends,
No sound to hear, no eye to see.
No words to write, my story ends,
Your distant tune my reverie.

And on the air the bells will peal.
And this broken heart will never heal.

69
THE RISING TIDE

We built a sandcastle on the beach,
Right here, I'm certain.
We dug, and molded the sand
For an entire day,
Until our backs were sore
And our skin was Caribbean-fried.
But it's gone.
Why can't we see it?
It was more than four feet tall
And three feet wide,
The biggest castle ever built,
A towering monument here
In the kingdom of little girls
Where the kindly king rules
And the young princess goes to hide.
But today the little girl will learn
That the kindly king has been deposed.
The castle of sand,
The fortress we built to last one thousand years,
Has fallen apart,
Washed away in the rising of the tide.

And in an instant
The little girl is gone.
Where did she go?
Why can't I see her?
She was right here with me,
On the beach, I am certain,
Standing by my side.
I turned my head for an instant
And she vanished,
Pulled away by forces I couldn't understand,
Though the heavens know I tried.
She was here then gone,
Her footprints in the sand
Washed away, erased completely,
The evidence vanished
As if she had something to hide.
The relentless waves washed against my feet
As I set the sun
And counted the times she played with me,
Stayed with me,
stood with me,
Built castles with me.
The steady cadence of rolling water,
Kept a tally
Of our adventures, our make-believes,
The hundred ways I could make her laugh,
Ten-thousand tears I dried.
And though she was struck with wanderlust
I urged, stay with me.

Lean on me,

Hold on to me

Until you hit your stride.

I have so much more to teach you,

Show you,

Share with you.

Stay very close to me,

Let me be your guide,

Then came the waves,

Fierce, unrelenting,

Pulling, pushing.

The castle wasn't big enough,

The beach was too small,

The world was too small,

And she seemed distant,

Beyond the flat horizon,

Far away, preoccupied.

And she knew there were other seas yet to cross,

Other lands,

New horizons,

Other castles to build.

As I offered her my hand

She gently pushed it aside,

And confidently said, "I know where I'm going.

You showed me the tidal pools,

The underwater life washed ashore,

New creatures in the outdoor school,

So many things I'd never seen before.

And I'm glad you woke me at exactly five-fifteen--

The charts said would be low tide--

And I thank you for the starfish,

For the spider crabs and the anemone,

And I thank you for taking me with you on this journey,

It's been quite a ride.

But now it's time for me to leave.

I know what I'm doing,

I know where I'm going,

And it's time for you to let me go,

Time to let me decide."

She handed me the yellow bucket,

The red plastic shovel,

And said, "I'm through with these."

And in her confident eyes

I could see that she was off,

Off to find new beaches, new horizons.

I could feel her restlessness,

Standing in the cool of the amber dawn

Like the retreating waves,

This restless spirit was already gone.

And I knew, she knew

That she may never change the world,

Build castles,

Erect monuments,

Rule kingdoms,

Or re-order the stars.

But I knew, she knew

That by walking the rocky shoals at sunrise,

She would find new life she hadn't seen before,

That she would see the world with new eyes,

That she would find a lasting cadence,

Find her own pace, her own rhythm.

Conquer her worst fears,

Defeat villains and hated foes.

Then meet me on the beach,

Leave footprints in the sand

And feel, once again,

The coolness of the earth between her toes.

And now she takes my hand

And listens to the unspoken words I have to say:

"Whether you rise or fall,

Whether you're leaving again,

Or, for just a little while, you're here to stay,

Whether you come or go,

Plant your feet or wash away,

Whether you choose to leave me alone

Or remain here at my side,

I won't stand in your way.

I have no power to calm the water,

No strength to stop the waves--

Though heaven knows I've tried.

I celebrate your strength,

A victim of the spinning globe,

A defiant addict of gravity

Who comes and goes in a foamy instant--

The pull of the moon,

The rising of the tide.

70

MRS. WRAY

Thank you kindly Mrs. Wray.
When I was seventeen,
There were so many things I didn't see or hear,
So many voices I didn't know were speaking,
Or how to understand all the things
They were trying to say.

You were hard on me most of the time,
Or so it seemed to me back then.
"It's just not good enough," she would say.
"You're a better writer than this,
I'm certain you can improve it,
Now sit down and try again."

Giving me more C's than B's--
How could I know you were molding me like clay--
As I doubted, as I struggled to express myself,
To find my voice,
The tinny voice of a tangled teen,
And write the things I longed to say.

Now more than fifty years later,
I've gleaned a few insights
And a little wisdom, I hope and pray.
But let it be said after all of this,
Let others take note
As distant voices fade away.

That at least one young man remembered
The pretty, red-haired English teacher
Who wouldn't let him quit,
As he callously pushed so many other things aside,
That at least he kept on writing,
At the very least he tried.

I'm still sitting alone at my desk
Working on my writing, most mornings
At about a B-minus level I would have to say.
But for the way you believed in me,
After more than half a century,
I thank you most kindly Mrs. Wray.

DESIGN & PAGINATION BY PRESERVATION BOOKS
PO BOX 95274 SOUTH JORDAN, UT 84095-0274
www.preservationbooks.com

Made in the USA
Columbia, SC
27 July 2024

39408234R00159